Her Write HIS NAME

THOEMMES

For David

SHELLS FROM THE SANDS OF TIME

Rosina Bulwer Lytton

With a new Introduction by
Marie Mulvey Roberts

THOEMMES PRESS

Published in 1995 by

Thoemmes Press
11 Great George Street
Bristol BS1 5RR
England

ISBN 1 85506 386 7

This is a reprint of the 1876 Edition
© Introduction by Marie Mulvey Roberts 1995

Publisher's Note

These reprints are taken from original copies of each book. In many cases the condition of those originals is not perfect, the paper, often handmade, having suffered over time and the copy from such things as inconsistent printing pressures resulting in faint text, show-through from one side of a leaf to the other, the filling in of some characters, and the break up of type. The publisher has gone to great lengths to ensure the quality of these reprints but points out that certain characteristics of the original copies will, of necessity, be apparent in reprints thereof.

My Epitaph

Long has been the way, and very dreary,
With heavy clouds of blackest wrongs o'ercast;
But the pilgrim, spent and weary,
Gladly sees the goal at last.

When Death o'erthrow the glass of time,
He scatters all its sands of sorrow;
And the freed soul doth upward climb
To welcome God's eternal morrow.

Rosina Bulwer Lytton

ACKNOWLEDGEMENTS

I would like to thank Clare Fleck, Jo Birch and the staff at the Estate Office at Knebworth House for all their help and enthusiasm. Acknowledgement goes to the staff at the Hertfordshire Record Office especially Kathryn Thompson for their assistance. Special thanks are due to David Cobbold for his encouragement and support. I would also like to thank Helen Boden, Kate Docker, Sandi Fish, Clare Fleck, Marion Glastonbury, Naomi Lester, Mary Links, Helen Small and John Charles Smith for commenting on my introduction.

INTRODUCTION

By the time Rosina Bulwer Lytton's last full-length book, the collection of essays called *Shells from the Sands of Time*, appeared in 1876, she had written over a dozen novels. In spite of this productivity, she has been noted less for her literary achievements than for the notoriety of her tempestuous marriage to the politician and novelist, Sir Edward Bulwer-Lytton. Nevertheless, she subverted her role as a wife by turning it into a position of protest from which she drew attention to the powerlessness of married women. Far from being subsumed by her husband's identity and family name, Rosina Bulwer Lytton went on to appropriate his surname as a banner for her war against marriage.[1] Having taken his name in matrimony, she discovered how effectively it could be used against her. A woman's nuptial renaming signified the loss of her personhood as recognized in law. Husbands, such as William Thackeray and Edward Bulwer-Lytton, took advantage of the authority that their conjugal contract had vested in them by joining with male doctors to authorize their respective wife's committal to a lunatic asylum.

Much as she detested the family name and title, Rosina Bulwer Lytton had no compunction in trading

---

[1] Sibylla Jane Flower pointed out to me that before the death of his mother, Edward Bulwer-Lytton was called Edward Lytton Bulwer. Whether there should be the hyphen that is commonly used is open to doubt as Edward never used one. His wife was called Rosina Lytton Bulwer and after 1843 became known as Rosina Bulwer Lytton.

on that which she was seeking to discredit. In a letter to her publisher dated January 20, 1851 about her new novel, *Miriam Sedley* (1850) she admits, 'I am also perfectly aware that my books are a very good speculation to any publisher, as the name alone sells them...'.[2] That her husband's novels sold well and were held in almost as high esteem in some quarters as those of his friend and fellow-novelist, Charles Dickens, would not have escaped her notice. It is likely that she had calculated to capitalize on his success by marketing her own fiction, even if this meant competing with him for sales. With titles like *Behind the Scenes* (1854), and *The World and His Wife, or a Person of Consequence, a Photographic Novel* (1858), these novels held out the promise of an intimate exposure of the private lives of public figures. While Edward Bulwer-Lytton's novels provided Rosina with material to parody and pastiche, she drew upon her real-life experiences to show how conjugal bliss could turn into marital hell. Ill-treatments she claims to have suffered at his hands included the taking away of her children, physical and mental cruelty and the humiliation of his numerous infidelities. His cruellest act was to have her confined in Brentford at Inverness Lodge, which was an institution for the mentally defective, because of her failure to carry out her wifely duties.

In some episodes of her fiction, where she dramatizes her suffering, she cannot resist portraying herself as a romantic, long-suffering, raven-haired beauty, while demonizing Edward Bulwer-Lytton as a villain and persecutor. Since she did not want to provide him with any incentive for taking out a libel suit against her, she adopts disguised names. Despite this precaution, one

[2] Louisa Devey, *Life of Rosina, Lady Lytton* (London: Sonnenschein, 1887), pp. 252–3.

can often identify the real-life template from which the fictional characters are drawn. For example, she lampoons Edward Bulwer-Lytton and his family seat at Knebworth by dedicating the preface of her most acclaimed novel, *Cheveley* (1839) 'TO NO ONE NOBODY, Esq., of NO HALL, NOWHERE'.[3] Here she strips him of all that is most precious, namely, his title, family name and the ancestral heritage of his home. This negative dedication sets the tone of a novel that was written in the wake of her disillusionment with her husband, underscored by the ironic subtitle, *The Man of Honour*.

It is likely that Edward Bulwer-Lytton, not to be outdone, was the author of a poem written to defend his honour. Published anonymously, it carried the title of *Lady Cheveley or, The Woman of Honour* and was subtitled *A New Version of Cheveley or, The Man of Honour* (1839). Even though the parodic nature of the verse is evident from the title, the subtitle is ambivalent in that it could mislead an unsuspecting reader into supposing that Rosina Bulwer Lytton, who was given to self-parody, was the actual poet. Continuing the saga of the embattled pair, this poem could be seen as the latest bid to lure away her readers in retaliation for the attempts she had made to win over his readership. The 'new version' of *Cheveley* had been written to warn husbands of how an errant wife can betray her 'lord's' name:

Oh! when you find in her who bears your name,
The cold remorseless sland'rer of your fame,
Then if you grieve, grieve silent and alone,
Nor seek the sympathy you have not shewn!

---

[3] Rosina Bulwer Lytton, *Cheveley: or, The Man of Honour*, 3 volumes (London: Bull, 1839), preface.

> Remember that you smiled, a wife to find, –
> Unblushing own the adultery of the mind,
> Who dipped her brush in gall to paint her lord.[4]

In a footnote, the poet accuses the wife of being stained with the sin of committing adultery in her mind. Considering that Edward Bulwer-Lytton's adultery was conspicuously corporeal, then, if he be the author, this condemnation smacks of hypocrisy. Readers who had dared to 'smile upon that venomed page/A lasting blot upon a maudlin age'[5] were accused, not only for having blotted their own moral copy book, but also for colluding with her treachery.

> Smile while the traitor wife, the fire-side spy,
> Weaves the base slander, and the specious lie,...
> Oh! while a wife with matricidal dart
> Would strike a husband through his mother's heart:
> Then, if you spurn her not, with one acclaim,
> You share her matchless sin, her deathless shame![6]

The above also refers to the hostility between Rosina Bulwer Lytton and her mother-in-law. The vituperation is no less remorseless when the poet turns his attention to the characters in *Cheveley*. Here, the widowed heroine is castigated for allowing herself to be distracted from her bereavement for her dead husband by another man:

> Remember when she dared her page defile
> With Cheveley's prosing love and dastard wile,
> And closed the scene, as though all shame to brave,

4   Anonymous, *Lady Cheveley or, The Woman of Honour. A New Version of Cheveley: or, The Man of Honour* (London: Churton, 1839), pp. 20–1.

5   *ibid.*, p. 15.

6   *ibid.*, pp. 15–16.

> Sporting with Cheveley o'er her husband's grave!
> You scarcely shuddered at the sick'ning view;
> 'Twas very bad – but what was that to you?
> Yet truth is truth, that deadly web was wrought
> Out of the venom of a woman's thought.[7]

The attentions of the authoress can be read in the above, as being diverted more forcibly from her dead husband by the novel *Cheveley* than by the eponymous hero. Edward probably anticipated that, after his death, Rosina would no more respect the role of sorrowful widow than she had venerated that of the dutiful wife. In her 'Last Will and Testament', she treats the title 'widow' as synonymous with 'freed woman'. Her own epitaph, which is reproduced near the beginning of this book along with the verses quoted below, obliquely refers to her marital sufferings, and she had wanted this to be engraved upon her gravestone. At a time when divorce was difficult for women to obtain, the death of a spouse was often the only decree absolute available to them.[8] Among her papers is an irreverent epitaph to Edward Bulwer-Lytton, which is marked by her ebullient wit and spiked by a traditional Irish raillery. The extract from it in the jingle below refers to the financial flash-point between them. While he reprimanded her for being wilfully extravagant, she reproached him for being doggedly parsimonious. The pun on the word 'lies' is an echo of the notices with which she fly-posted parts of Hertfordshire in which

---

[7] *Lady Cheveley*, p. 22.

[8] Caroline Norton was another embattled wife who campaigned for the right of a wife to sue for divorce. Some of her suggestions to protect the rights of divorced and separated wives were included in The Marriage and Divorce Act passed in 1857. The Married Women's Property Act 1882 gave wives the right to their own property.

she bestowed upon her husband the new title of 'Sir Liar'.

Here, still lies, my Lord Lytton, – at last in a fix!
Being too stingy to pay, his fare o'er the Styx.[9]

This is contained in one of Rosina's letters to her son Robert where she warms to her theme with a barbed attack on the House of Lords, saying, even the devil does not know what to do with him, having no '"Upper House", wherein to shelve him'.[10] More damning than the levity of this comic rendition about her deceased husband bedevilling the devil is the scorching memoir, *A Blighted Life* (1880). Here, her naming of names exposed the then Dowager Lady Lytton to potentially ruinous litigation from the Bulwer-Lytton estate. Expediently, she denied that she had intended the text for publication and insisted that it had appeared in print without her permission.

Rosina Bulwer Lytton was aware of the dangers besetting a woman bold enough to trespass into the traditionally male print-culture. Even as a separated wife, her husband was empowered to confiscate the very royalties with which she was trying to gain some financial independence from him. If Edward Bulwer-Lytton had taken such action, he would have been in the anomalous position of having literally profited from his wife's thinly disguised fictional attacks. Instead, he tried to undermine her by more subtle methods. Rosina Bulwer Lytton was convinced that he had recruited hostile reviewers in order to discredit her novels. In *Very Successful* (1859), she describes these reviewers

---

[9] This is in the manuscript collection (D/EK C29/16) housed at the County Record Office, Hertfordshire.

[10] *ibid.*

as a 'literary inquisition'.[11] Her sense of being at war with the literary establishment, where Edward Bulwer-Lytton wielded considerable influence, is reinforced by the images of combat in her defiant and belligerent novel *Very Successful!* Here, for example, Sir Titaniferous Thompson can be found jousting. No less defensive is her preface to *Very Successful!* where she pre-empts the adverse criticism of those who she believed were more willing to attack her because she was a woman.

That Rosina Bulwer Lytton felt disadvantaged as a novelist by her sex is revealing when one considers how heavily women had invested in the novel, by this time, both as authors and readers. During the eighteenth century, the number of women novelists had outstripped their male counterparts, while female writers were still in vogue during the Victorian period. Men, writing in the last century's cult of sensibility, were known to have occasionally used female pseudonyms in order to boost sales. The situation had reversed by the following century so that women, such as Rosina Bulwer Lytton, sometimes used a male *nom de plume*.[12] The reason why some women published under a male name was because they were aware that, in some quarters, novel writing had become an even greater affront than before to feminine decorum. In *Cheveley*, Rosina Bulwer Lytton debunks the belief that literature was open equally to women and to men, saying:

[11] This is included in the notice at the beginning of *Very Successful!*, 3 volumes (London: Whittaker, 1856).

[12] For novels written towards the end of her life Rosina Bulwer Lytton used the pen-name of George Scott.

generally speaking, women have either fathers, brothers, or husbands, who would shrink from having an authoress for a daughter, sister, or wife; and the reason is obvious: it arises from a fear that they might either disgrace or distinguish themselves, – two results equally distasteful to the pride of man.[13]

Even the name of Anna Wheeler, Rosina's mother and a pioneer for women's rights, had not appeared, until recently, on the title-page of the tome she co-authored with William Thompson entitled *Appeal of One Half the Human Race, Women, Against the Pretensions of the Other Half, Men* (1825). The reason was that William Thompson had wanted her to publish a single authored text under her own name. Unfortunately, this had resulted in her not getting the credit she deserved for her contribution to the *Appeal*. Elsewhere, the Wollstonecraftian Anna Wheeler published a number of diatribes against marriage and the subordination of women under the name of 'Vlasta'. Such bitter observations as a woman may marry a man because 'he offers her no good excuse for hating him',[14] recall her own unhappy marriage.

Under her maiden name of Anna Doyle, she was courted by the dashing Francis Massy Wheeler, whom she met at the races. He was the grandson of a prominent landowner of County Limerick, whose Anglo-Irish ancestry is described thus by a member of his family: 'Titled Fools at the Conquest, and had continued uninterrupted so, without the plebeian taint

[13] Rosina Bulwer Lytton, *Cheveley*, volume 1, p. 215.

[14] *Vlasta*, [Anna Wheeler] in a letter to the editor of *The Crisis* for August 31, 1833 reproduced in *The Rebels: Irish Feminism and Nationalism*, editors, Marie Mulvey Roberts and Tamae Mizuta in *Controversies in the History of British Feminism* (Rouledge/Thoemmes, London, 1995).

of brains having come between them and their nobility.'[15]   The widowed Mrs Doyle opposed the match, but to no avail. The betrothal was announced when Anna was only fifteen years old and her fiance was four years older. Francis Doyle's alcoholism and idleness eventually drove her to desertion. She swept off her sister and two daughters, Rosina and Henrietta, and went to live with an uncle in Guernsey. In 1816 Anna Wheeler settled in France where she became the centre of one of the earliest Saint-Simonian circle. This was a group of radical communitarians, who challenged orthodox religion, the traditional family structure and the conventions of marriage through rational argument.

It is highly probable that for much of her account of courtship and marriage in a letter to the editor of *The Crisis*, Anna Wheeler was drawing upon her own marital miseries. She describes how a girl thrust upon the marriage market was subjected to a 'constant sense of degradation'.[16] Anna Wheeler, who was a stunning beauty, realized that attractive women were more likely to be pursued by 'sensual fools or selfish knaves'.[17] As a highly intelligent woman, she was able to commiserate with all learned wives who were married to a blockhead, dunce or drone 'who lounges before the fire, spitting into it like a roasting apple'.[18] She observed that, after marriage, a man's love (or sexual appetite) often diminishes whereas that of a woman can increase. In this case, devotion to a husband could amount to a 'humiliating idolatry'.[19] Anna Wheeler's most radical

[15] Quoted by Richard Pankhurst, 'Anna Wheeler: A Pioneer Socialist and Feminist', *The Political Quarterly* (1954), XXV, 133.

[16] Wheeler, *The Rebels*.

[17] *ibid.*

[18] *ibid.*

[19] *ibid.*

pronouncement on the subject was her declaration: 'I hold that woman's love is the symbol of her deep degradation, moral and social.'[20] The metaphor she chooses to describe such love is that of an 'incubus'. This is the name given to a sexualized and supernatural fiend on which were blamed some women's nightmares. It is an appropriate trope for her warning of how a bride can awaken from her trance of romantic love into a bad dream of married life. By the time Anna Wheeler wrote this attack on marriage, her own daughter had already awoken from the intoxication of courtship into six years of a toxic marriage. Miss Green, who took care of the Bulwer-Lyttons' children, recollects the advent of Rosina's disillusionment.[21] Prior to that, during the early part of their marriage, she had been inordinately devoted to her husband. Rosina Doyle Wheeler, who used both her mother's and father's names before entering wedlock, incurred the opposition of her bridegroom's widowed mother to her engagement to Edward Bulwer-Lytton. Mrs Bulwer, who was a forceful woman and used to having her way, nevertheless, did not succeed in preventing the marriage from going ahead on 19 August 1827. The change that Rosina experienced in Edward after the honeymoon may have inspired an episode in *Cheveley*. Here, the newly married Lady de Clifford is scolded by her husband for calling him by his Christian name. She had not realized that this was a familiarity permitted only during the honeymoon period and that married life required more formality. Lord de Clifford also ordered her never to feed his horse again since this was a task not fitting for

[20] Wheeler, *The Rebels*.

[21] See page 16 of Miss Green's unpublished Journal (Knebworth House Archives, Hertfordshire. Private collection).

the mistress of the house to carry out. Thinking that he was joking, she laughs only to realize how serious he is when he threatens to knock her down. The author satirically refers to Lady de Clifford as the ideal wife, in that she possesses the rarest quality of all, that of being able to adore her husband.

Naming, as in the example above, signifies how states can alter in privacy as well as in public. But the dichotomy between the private and the public has been the site of the double-standard, having operated, invariably, to the advantage of men. Rosina Bulwer Lytton points out in *Cheveley* that private vices are often camouflaged by public virtues, and goes on to protest:

> With one man's pet sins, no other man has a right to interfere above all with the treatment of wives; for a wife is a man's own exclusive property, an ambulating chattel, for whose comparative value the law has recently established a tariff; for I read in the police report, a few days ago, that a fellow having severely beaten his wife, and his donkey on the same day, the worthy magistrate fined him fifteen shillings for the latter outrage, accompanied with a lecture on cruelty to animals; and added another five, for the former, but lesser misdemeanour....[22]

Wives, as a calumniated class, were confined to the domestic sphere, which Rosina Bulwer Lytton graphically describes as 'the conjugal treadmill'[23] in her novel *The School for Husbands* (1852). For these women, marriage was their martyrdom and the marital name was their stigmata:

[22] Bulwer Lytton, *Cheveley*, volume 3, p. 181.

[23] Bulwer Lytton, *The School for Husbands: or Moliére's Life and Times*, 3 volumes (London: Skeet, 1852), volume 1, p. 94.

how many uncanonised martyrs there are in every-day domestic life, hourly warring both with the flesh and the spirit (and literally taking up their cross daily); and this must ever be the case as long as men continue to enforce the laws of God grammatically, thereby assuming a wide difference between the masculine and the feminine.[24]

In order to show that men are capable of empathizing with women, Rosina Bulwer Lytton writes from the point of view of a sympathetic male character in *School for Husbands* (1852) about the way in which women are treated:

Women, by nature weaker than we are, from their more impressionable and susceptible organisation, we make still weaker, by fettering them from their birth with the swathings of inane conventionalities; for we cripple our women's minds, as the Chinese do their women's feet; we pen them in the narrow fold of irresponsibility, up to a certain point, never allowing them to think for themselves, or lean upon their own resources, denying them the wholesome mental food of rational beings. We sweeten the panada of their assumed inferiority, till we in reality enfeeble them...and then we throw them into that great arena of impossibilities, the world, to wrestle, single-handed, and unarmed with practised gladiators and untamed tigers.[25]

For many women, female education had not only failed to equip them for marital combat, but had barely enabled them to spell. In an appropriately pedagogical

[24] Bulwer Lytton, *Cheveley*, volume 1, p. 2.

[25] Bulwer Lytton, *School for Husbands*, volume 1, p. 184.

episode in the aptly entitled, *School for Husbands*, an Abbé undermines a woman's assertiveness by taking her to task over her spelling in a billet. After crumpling up her letter, he proceeds to crush the letter-writer:

> ...and you dare made such an assertion, Madame, in the teeth of three grammatical errors, and five misspelt words...for what independence could I place on a woman who has no fixed principle of grammar, and turns the alphabet into a raffle.[26]

Grammar here is turned into oppression; the masculine monologic dominating the feminine heteroglossic of women's lives. In 'An Essay upon Essays', Rosina Bulwer Lytton argues that woman's mission, which the dominant ideology identified as submissiveness to her husband, ought to be the same as a man's mission. It had been in the interests of male hegemony to keep women as docile and ill-informed as possible. In the same way as Mary Wollstonecraft castigates middle-class women for their indolence, Rosina Bulwer Lytton reproaches them for their ignorance, saying:

> Now don't let any woman who does me the honour of reading these pages suppose for one moment that I am preaching up the limited liability household drudge system for women. God forbid! In a general way, it is their ignorance that is their infirmity, the more they know...the more they'll do and the better they'll be. (p. 123)[27]

In the autobiographical novel, *Miriam Sedley* (1850), Rosina Bulwer Lytton criticizes the inadequacy of

---

[26] Bulwer Lytton, *School for Husbands*, volume 2, p. 235.

[27] Page numbers in brackets after quotations refer to *Shells From the Sands of Time*.

education for girls. The eponymous heroine from Ireland goes to a school for young ladies in England and horrifies her teacher by speaking Irish. In a jibe against the English monoglot culture, Miriam admits that while abroad, her education has been neglected since she had learned so many languages. One of the languages Rosina Bulwer Lytton could speak was French, having lived in Guernsey with her mother, where she mingled with refugees fleeing the French Revolution. Her visits to France enabled her to cultivate a love for French culture and literature. In the 'Essay upon Essays' in *Shells from the Sands of Time*, Rosina Bulwer Lytton praises Montaigne as her greatest hero.[28] In her essay 'Happy Jack', the English are compared unfavourably with the French:

> There can be no doubt that the flatness, staleness, unprofitableness, and inanity of English life arise from its block machinery sort of uniformity, and total want of individuality in thought, action, or character; its echo and follow-my-leader sort of conventionality; which causes anything like originality or independence of opinion or action, in the rash perpetrator of either, to pass for mad or bad; and be tabooed accordingly. (p. 164)

The essayist herself had been shunned by society after breaking the cultural codes governing femininity, for which she was condemned as both mad and bad. In the same essay, she complains that flagrant vices were often cited as 'proofs of genius and superiority'. This agenda is clearly gendered, since the flagrant vices to which she refers were those practised by men and inculcated

---

[28] References to this text are in brackets following quotes. Even though she could read French, Rosina Bulwer Lytton probably read Montaigne in English since his French was so archaic.

within the English public school system. In her novel, *The Peer's Daughters* (1849), the deficiencies of education for boys are itemized:

> A young gentleman, after he has had his selfishness put into a hot-bed by the injudicious indulgence of his mamma, and his temper, which nature had merely made hasty, hardened into tyranny, by his constant and unchecked domineering over his sisters, in the tread-mill of his own nursery, is then drafted off to the educational galleys of a public school, where he runs the gauntlet of every embryo vice, till he is old enough to go to college, to perfectionise and confirm them.[29]

For this passage Rosina may have had Edward's schooling in mind and his pampering as a boy by his mother. There was later little opportunity for her to pamper her only son, Robert, to whom, she claimed, she had been given the minimum access after her formal separation from her husband in 1836. In her prayer book, which has been discovered recently at Knebworth House, there is an angry retort to her son Robert, 'When I am dead, never act by Any, as you have done by your mother'.[30] She suffered acutely from the estrangement of her children, particularly the loss of her daughter, Emily, who died lonely and neglected at the age of nineteen from typhoid fever. Pasted inside the prayer book is a poignant little poem called 'The Little Grave' by Rowland Brown. This may have given her some solace along with one of the ghost stories in *Shells From the Sands of Time*, which is about a flaxen-haired girl whose apparition bears a resemblance to the

[29] *The Peer's Daughters: A Novel*, 3 volumes (London: T. C. Newby, 1849), volume 2, p. 193.

[30] The prayer book is housed at Knebworth House Archives, Hertfordshire. The words quoted appear on the front inside cover.

young Emily, who had been known as a child as 'Little Boots'. Mistaken for a sprite by an inquisitive colonel, the central character is, in fact, the ghost of a child who had drowned.

Edward Bulwer-Lytton also wrote ghost stories, the most famous of which is 'The Haunted and the Haunters' (1857). In pursuit of his interest in spiritualism and psychic research, he invited the medium, Daniel Dunglas Home to stay with him at Knebworth House. Curiosity about the mysteries of the after-life prompted him to attend a necromantic ritual upon a roof of a shop in Regent Street in London for the purpose of summoning Apollonius of Tyana, who was a first century Pythagorean sage. More sinister are the seances through which Edward Bulwer-Lytton tried to communicate with the spirit of his dead daughter.[31] It would seem that Emily's parents were being haunted by their neglect of her. True to form, each blamed the other for her premature demise. Edward accused Rosina of hastening her death by visiting her dying daughter, while Rosina, in a letter of January 30, 1854 to the Chevalier de Berrat, accused Edward of murdering Emily by working her too hard as a domestic servant.

At the back of Rosina Bulwer Lytton's prayer-book is written a bleak note of despair: 'Too late the hope that was my life, is dead.' Little wonder that she had called her memoirs *A Blighted Life*. She can be seen to have been blighted and thwarted not only in life but also in death. It is almost as though she had anticipated correctly that she would be buried in an unmarked

---

[31] See Harold Armitage's introduction to Edward Bulwer-Lytton, *The Haunted and the Haunters* (London: Simpkin, Marshall, Hamilton, Kent, 1925), p. 10.

grave, when she pasted the following words in her prayer-book:

> All eyes survey upon the coffin the records of names, of sex, of age, and the day of departure from earth – records how useless! and dropped into darkness as if messages addressed to worms.

After she died, at the age of eighty, no-one put a headstone on her grave with the inscription that she had requested in her will: 'The Lord shall give thee rest from thy sorrow, and from thy fear, and from the hard bondage wherein thou wast made to serve' (Isaiah, xiv. 3).[32]   Over a hundred years later following her death in 1882, her last wishes were carried out. On the anniversary of her death, March 12 1995, her great-great grandson, Lord Cobbold arranged for a tombstone to be erected on her grave in the churchyard of St John the Evangelist at Shirley in Surrey. The sense of her own mortality was doubtless why Rosina Bulwer Lytton included in her prayer-book the verses called 'The Sands of Human Race':

> One by one the sands are flowing,
> One by one the moments fall;
> Some are coming, some are going –
> Do not strive to grasp them all....
>
> Do not linger with regretting,
> Or for passion's hour despond;
> Nor the daily hour forgetting
> Look too eagerly beyond.

---

[32] See Devey, *Life of Rosina*, p. 427. Later, Rosina Bulwer Lytton abandoned the romantic idea requested in her first will that, after her death, her heart be removed, embalmed and then sent as a letter (*ibid.*, p. 425).

> Hours are golden links – God's token –
> Reaching Heaven; but, one by one,
> Taken them, lest the chain be broken,
> Ere the pilgrimage be done.

That *Shells from the Sands of Time* was written as she neared her death, is indicative of how she was reflecting upon her life and the influences that had shaped her thinking. The use of the old-fashioned long 's' that appears in the original text reproduced here may have been intended to convey a sense of the past. Looking back at some of the mentors who had inspired her, she states that 'the world, or rather human nature, never outgrows its Shakespeares, Senecas, Montaignes; because such minds are the pulses and arteries of its great universal heart' (pp. 132–3) and that 'The truly great are those, not whose writings make us wiser in the world's shallow lore, but those whose lives make us better.' (p. 131.)

Although Rosina's life may not have been so exemplary as that of her beloved Montaigne, it was certainly extraordinary. In her rejection of the subordination of women, she drew attention to the way in which husbands could exploit their wives. For example, in her novel, *Very Successful* she condemns marriage in no uncertain terms as 'a blasphemous, one-sided mockery, a saturnalia for men, and a Draco-like tyranny against women'.[33] For her dazzling wit[34] and the intensity of her polemical, highly idiosyncratic and controversial novels, she deserves far more recognition. This collection of essays reveals another side to the

[33] Bulwer Lytton, *Very Successful*, volume 3, p. 36.

[34] For an example of her wit see Rosina Bulwer Lytton, *A Blighted Life: A True Story*, with a new introduction by Marie Mulvey Roberts (Bristol: Thommes Press, 1994), p. xv.

character. They show her to be a woman who was widely read and highly educated, and whose immense talents are brought to bear on literature and philosophy. They may even give us a truer picture of the author than is reflected elsewhere in her writings, particularly if we agree with her declaration in 'An Essay upon Essays' that: 'If there be such a thing as sincerity in authors or truth in books, essay writing is unquestionably the truest and most sincere of any species of composition' (p. 112).

Marie Mulvey Roberts
University of the West of England, 1995

WORKS BY
ROSINA BULWER LYTTON

Cheveley: or, The Man of Honour, 3 volumes (London: Bull, 1839)

The Budget of the Bubble Family, 3 volumes (London: Bull, 1840)

The Prince-Duke and the Page: An Historical Novel, 3 volumes (London: Boone, 1841)

Bianca Cappello: An Historical Romance, 3 volumes (London: Bull, 1843)

Memoirs of a Muscovite, 3 volumes (London: Newby, 1844)

The Peer's Daughters: A Novel, 3 volumes (London: Newby, 1849)

Miriam Sedley, or The Tares and the Wheat: A Tale of Real Life, 3 volumes (London: Newby, 1850)

The School for Husbands: or Moliére's Life and Times, 3 volumes (London: Skeet, 1852)

Behind the Scenes, A Novel, 3 volumes (London: Skeet, 1854)

The World and his Wife, or a Person of Consequence, a Photographic novel, 3 volumes (London: Whittaker, 1858)

Very Successful! 3 volumes (London: Whittaker, 1859)

Where there's a Will there's a Way (Published anonymously, no date)

Clumber Chase by Hon. George Scott (Published anonymously, 1871)

Maulever's Divorce by Hon. George Scott (Published anonymously, 1871)

The Household Fairy (London: Hale, 1870)

Shells from the Sands of Time (London: Bickers, 1876)

A Blighted Life (London: London Publishing Office, 1880)

Refutation of an Audacious Forgery of the Dowager Lady's name to a book of the Publication of which she was totally Ignorant (Privately printed, 1880)

Water-colour of Rosina Bulwer Lytton
reproduced by kind permission of Lord Cobbold

There is no date or name of artist in the
Knebworth brochure from whence it came

SHELLS FROM THE SANDS

OF TIME.

BY

THE DOWAGER LADY LYTTON.

LONDON

BICKERS AND SON, I, LEICESTER SQUARE.

1876.

CHISWICK PRESS:—PRINTED BY WHITTINGHAM AND WILKINS,
TOOKS COURT, CHANCERY LANE.

CONTENTS.

ON BAD MANNERS.

UR friend, the German poet, hiſ-
torian, metaphyſician, and portrait
painter, quoted by Burton, but
whoſe name, unfortunately (not to
ſay unfairly), has not deſcended to poſterity,
by his revelations about England, reminds us
of the debt of gratitude we ſtill continue to
incur to " diſtinguiſhed foreigners," for eternally
pointing out to us mines of vice and mountains
of virtue which, without their kind intervention,
our own indigenous perceptions would neither
have been ſufficiently elevated nor profound to
have diſcovered; and even when they note a
palpable and indiſputable fact, they generally
prop it up with an auxiliary or mine it with a
motive that we natives ignored before. Thus,
the French *will* have it to this day, that Engliſh
women are inſanely *romantic*, it has even paſſed
into a proverb with them—*romaneſque comme une*

Anglaise:" and as they are the only people who go to war for an idea, ſo are they the only people who generouſly and gratuitouſly graft their ideas on the numſkulls of other nations, and in ſo doing, they have decided that this "given" romantic mania of Engliſh women has its origin in tea, toaſt, green veils, and grooms ; that is, from an over-indulgence in the three former, and from young ladies (*des jeunes "meeſſes"*.) being allowed to ride out *ſola* with the latter. This was the ſtereotyped French theory of the eighteenth century, and neither the intercourſe of a ſixty or forty years' peace, nor a conſequently nearer view of, and more intimate acquaintance with, bottled porter, beef-ſteaks, and Balmoral boots, has at all been able to diſpel this "romantic" idea from French brains. The next chimera, not only of the French, but of moſt continental peoples, is the exceeding domeſticity and love of home of the *male* as well as the female ſpecimen of the Anglo-Saxon. They have an *idée fixe* that even *mi Lord Bull,* in the higheſt claſſes, is benevolently addicted to balancing his own babies, while my Lady Bull is equally perſevering in ſewing on ſhirt buttons, and offering her maſter the deferential homage of a ſilent admiration,—in ſhort, that an Engliſhman, like a ſnail, can with difficulty be got to protrude his head beyond his houfe, as is clearly demonftrated by our Clubs, ceafelefs continental tours, and univerfal *domophobia* in the upper claffes; and the gin-palace, the tap-room, and the "ring," in the lower. But Henrich Heine, in his "RIEISBILDER," is kind enough to point out the *caufe* of this exceeding ftay-at-homeativenefs among Englifhmen; and here it is, in all its ftartling novelty and profundity:—" L'Anglais cherche cette fatiffaction de l'âme (dans fon intérieur) que fa gaucherie naturelle, fous le rapport focial, lui interdit hors de chez-lui."[1]

It is certain that good manners are our national deficiency, and bad ones, our national curfe. This is fo patent, that marvels are made of the few exceptions that prove the rule, and we conftantly hear, as a noticeable and memorable thing, after a brief *réfumé* of a perfon's focial virtues or fhortcomings, as the cafe may be,—" But then Lady ——, Lord ——, Mr. This, or Mrs. That, have fuch charming manners," as in other countries perfons are cited for their fcientific or artiftic attainments. Nor does this *gaucherie*, fhynefs,

---

1 " An Englifhman feeks that internal felf-complacency at his own firefide which his natural awkwardnefs of manner in regard to all focial intercourfe precludes his enjoying beyond his own family circle." Granted the awkwardnefs of manner, but denied that it takes refuge in, and confines itfelf to, its own chimney-corner. Would that it did!

or whatever you choofe to call it, fo much origi-nate in pride, as in felfifhnefs. An Englifhman's firft dread, in extending a civility, or venturing upon anything like acquaintancefhip with ftrangers, is, that it *may* by fome remote poffibility entail boredom upon him of fome fort; and from his earlieft dawn the Anglo-Saxon has been in the habit of referring every-thing to felf, and never troubling his head what effect that very difagreeable autocrat may pro-duce upon others; hence, the ill breeding and, in many inftances, pofitive bearifhnefs of bro-thers and fons to their mothers and fifters, and of hufbands to their wives and daughters. And what we have not in our own homes, depend up-on it, we cannot take out into the world with us; and though a more gracious and courteous bearing may now and then be borrowed, like plate or jewels, for fome fpecial occafion, they are not *ours*, and form no part of us. The root of good breeding is Chriftianity; and the effence of genuine Chriftianity is *gratuitous and difin-terefted kindnefs*. If among all our job com-miffionerfhips we only had commiffioners of good breeding, and its evidence, good manners, the only teft they could poffibly obtain for the difcovery of real gentlemen and gentlewomen would be to fee them (unknown to the faid gentlemen and gentlewomen) with their inferiors, or with thofe who were under obligations to them, or who wanted their fervices. For as the devil can quote Scripture to further his own ends, fo even the moft felfifh and ill-bred perfons can be the moft amiable, *empreffé*, and *prévenant*, if they have a point to carry ; but the point once carried, the boundary wall once fcaled, fuch per-fons are apt to kick down the ladder too foon, never recollecting that it might again be *wanted* at fome future time ; for it is part of the fubtle chemiftry of God's retributive juftice that nothing fhould be fo narrow and fhort-fighted as Selfifh-nefs,—that ftrange, many-handed, no-hearted monfter, which is at once the parent and the offspring of every vice.

In a quaint old book, tranflated into Englifh in 1730, and written by one DON BALTASAR GRATIAN, the Locke of Spain, entitled "The Compleat Gentleman, or a Defcription of the feveral Qualifications, both Natural and Acquired, that are neceffary to form a Great Man," and dedicated by the tranflator (Mr. T. Saldkeld) to John Lord Boyle, among much heavy rubbifh in the way of ftyle, and rufty allegories, which were the knowledge vehicles then in vogue, there are many gems. And yet, perhaps, one has no right to complain of this circumlocution, for if it were the mere pith of the matter we wanted, the leaft thinking amongft us are, hourly and daily feeling, acting, and uttering, condensed into a proverb, some one of those truths which are elaborated in, and diffused over, an essay. Don Baltasar was evidently a man possessing great practical knowledge of the world, and as such was duly imbued with that great truth, constituting the first principles of social intercourse, that—

> Manners make the man, want of them the fellow,
> And all the rest is leather and prunella.

I shall therefore give, *in extenso*, his notions upon this all-important point, as set forth in a letter addressed to his friend Don Bartholomew de Morlanes.

"That maxim, *A manner in all things*, ought to be, dear Morlanes, one of the first you should study to practise, since Cleobulus was ranked amongst the wise men of the first class for only having taught it. Not to injure that philosopher, or wrong the judgment of antiquity, that has honoured him with so excellent a name, I should think it infinitely more glorious to practise a thorough regularity and decency of behaviour, than to teach it in the most flourishing academy. To know how to prescribe excellent rules, and nothing more, is to be only a simple rhetorician ; but to teach, and to practise what one teaches, is to be a philosopher in earnest ; *that* entitles one firstly to the denomination of a philosopher and wise man in the true fenfe of the words. Be that as it will, *A manner in everything* is one of the acknowledged maxims neceffary in practice; as there are certain principles allowed as felf-evident in fpeculation. No; a man fhould never be negligent about the MANNER in any matter whatfoever; for the MAN-NER is that which is always moft obvious and vifible; 'tis the outfide, the mark, the fign, and the fpecification, as it were, of the THING. By that external we come to the knowledge of the internal; by the *rine* [rind] and outfide of the fruit, which is vifible to the eye, we conjecture and judge of its nature and quality. A man likewife, whom we never faw in our lives, makes himfelf known to us in fome meafure by his air and his figure. Thus, is a manner fo far from being an indifferent circumftance with refpect to merit, that it is the very thing which notifies it to our fenfes, 'tis that which roufes our attention and engages it towards an object that has already been capable of pleafing us at firft fight. This fort of perfec-tion (for a perfection it is) comes within the reach and capacity of all people,[1] confequently,

---

[1] No, verily, Don Baltafar, it does *not*, for, like poets, they muft be "to the manner *born*." But what *does* come within the reach of all, with care and attention, if they would only put afide their felfifhnefs and doff their felf-conceit, is to be a little lefs ill-bred, by being more mindful of the feelings, or even it may be of the prejudices, of others.

it is unpardonable to renounce it, whatever fome pretenders to folidity may allege, who look upon manner as a trifling, inconfiderable circumftance. Some perfons are born with happy difpofitions for the acquiring of this talent, but yet they will never have it in perfection unlefs they themfelves fecond the advances that nature has made in their favour. There are others who have no previous difpofitions towards this talent ; thefe muft remedy that difadvantage by their own induftry ; art will, at leaft in fome meafure, fupply the defect of their natural deficiency. But when Nature in this refpect is feconded by Art and application, from that union will proceed a merit that charms mankind, a *je ne fçay quoy*,[1] an inexpreffible fomething that adorns our actions, beautifies our perfons, and ennobles nobility itfelf. Truth indeed has its force, Reason its power, and Justice its authority ; but every one of thefe lofes much of its value if it be not fet off and adorned with a becoming manner, but if they be accompanied by a fuitable manner, how greatly then is their value enhanced ! The charm of manner does yet more : it fupplies the very place of a thing itfelf, and compenfates for the meannefs or defect of it. It gives ftrength to a feeble truth, depth to a fuperficial reafon, and weight to

---

[1] Je ne fais quoi.

an infufficient authority. It even makes us forget
—what do I fay? it actually covers and razes—
that is too little ftill—it graces and adorns the
imperfections of Nature, and makes amends for
the niggard portion fhe has given us. In a word,
Manner is a kind of univerfal fupply that fur-
nifhes us with every thing we want. How many
affairs have been fpoiled and ruined by a difagreeable manner and behaviour, and how many, on
the other hand, have been profperous and fuccefsful, folely through the advantage of an agreeable deportment!

"The monarch's power, the ftatefman's aftute-
nefs, the general's bravery, the fcholar's learning,
are all imperfect qualities, if they be deftitute of
a fuitably graceful demeanour; but this equivalent,
enhancing attribute (if I may fo exprefs it), becomes a fubftantial, effential perfection, in thofe
perfons who are born to govern, or chofen to
command. Generally fpeaking, all fuperiors gain
more refpect and deference by condefcenfion and
humanity than by demanding or exacting them
in a defpotic or imperious way; and a fovereign
in particular, who fhades his greatnefs with an air
of kindnefs and benevolence, doubly engages us
to do our duty. By that means he reigns in our
hearts, and confequently over all the reft.

"In fhort, Manner is in all conditions and
fituations, an irrefiftible attraction and engage-

ment; it procures good-will at firſt ſight, and after having made that ſtep, it advances by degrees, and gains eſteem, and by theſe progreſſive motions it riſes at laſt to encomiums and applauſe. We ought, therefore, as I before ſaid, to omit no means or pains whatſoever, towards the forming of this talent, if Nature has not implanted it in us; for after all, they that are pleaſed with it (and who is there, that is not?) do not inquire whether it be natural or acquired; they reliſh the pleaſure of it, without any further examination or inquiry.

" MANNER,[1] in regard to the productions of wit and underſtanding, is almoſt a fundamental point. In the firſt place, if any piece of literature be grown antiquated, or ſunk into oblivion or obſcurity, or neglected and thrown by, from having been writ by an unſkilful author, this talent alone will bring it out of that ignominy and obſcurity into light, with honour and advantage. It reforms the antique groſſneſs of ſuch pieces, that would be offenſive to the modern politeneſs; it trims and dreſſes 'em up ſo agreeably, that the world receives them with as much applauſe as if they were new products of the writer's own genius.[2] But as we grow

---

[1] *i.e.* Style.

[2] Terrible encouragement (by no means wanted) for wholeſale plagiariſts, this!

every day more and more perfect, the present prevailing taste, you'll say, and not the ancient, is to be consulted, to surprise the modern reigning taste out of a superannuated composition, or old-fashioned treatise. A small alteration is often sufficient for that purpose, some little new turn, which disguises the old thought, and makes it pass for a new one.[1] Every thing seems to become new in some men's hands,[2] that have a certain peculiar cast of wit. With that talent they take out all that's flat in a mean author, all that is insipid in a trite subject, and all that's servile in an imitation. Let the matter they handle be what it will, historical or rhetorical, the historian will be read and the orator will be heard; for though the subject may be common, yet 'tis treated after a new and uncommon manner.

---

[1] Indeed! What a pity that this art, like that of painting on glass, should be lost to the present generation!

[2] As in those of the Mosaic-Arab gentlemen of Monmouth Street or the Minories, for instance, or as a politician's coat, however often turned, or even what may be called a gilt-gingerbread calibre of intellect, from the grotesque trashiness of its substratum, plastered on the surface with an ornate gorgeousness of glitter that amounts to vulgarity, may, with manner and temper combined, vanquish the fatal Hydra RIDICULE itself, which keeps watch and ward at the base of Ambition's very dirty slippery *mât de cocagne*, succeed in climbing it, and vigorously seize from its pinnacle the onerous burdens of its golden talismans of power and position.

" In the fecond place, things that are in themfelves choice and exquifite, 'tis true, do not
weary us, though they be prefented to our minds
over and over again. But yet if they do not
weary us, they at leaft ceafe to entertain us with
equal pleafure. Now this is the time we fhould
perceive it neceffary to have recourfe to the
magic of manner, and to give the fubject that
new drefs which it feems to require. The new
decoration ftrikes and awakens the fancy, and
pleafes it as much as if fome new objects were
prefented to it; whereas they are only the fame,
placed in a new and different light; old pictures
juft vamped up, and re-varnifhed. Thefe,
then, are two maxims conftantly true in matters
of literature: that, on the one hand, the moft
ingenious piece will not be pleafing to the tafte
if it be not feafoned and difhed up with an
agreeable manner, and, on the other hand, the
moft common or trivial thing is no longer fo,
if it be treated in a polite (!) way, in that engaging manner which new-models every thing it
takes in hand.

" A manner is likewife of great advantage in
civil fociety,[1] in the common, ordinary converfe
of life. Let two men relate the fame ftory: the

---

[1] So it is to be prefumed, for without good manners fociety,
were it called *la crême de la crême*, can fcarcely *be* civil.

one fhall pleafe, and the other difguft ; this is a wide difference, whence does it proceed ? Why, it proceeds entirely from the manner. The one has fomething in his air and manner that is either affecting, engaging, humorous, or *piquant*, the other has fomething awkward or dull in his perfon and language, which tires the hearers, or lulls them to fleep. But the worft of all is, when a man's manner and behaviour is not only not agreeable, but is pofitively bad and difagreeable, and that wilful and affected too, as is often the cafe with men in great pofts and employments. How many have we known whofe harfh, rude, infolent, brutifh manner has made all mankind avoid them ! 'Your haughty, fupercilious air,' faid a wife man once—to one that you and I know[1]—'is not indeed in itfelf a vice which ought to brand you with difhonour ; but neverthelefs, it is a fault, and fuch a confiderable

---

[1] The reader will have the goodnefs to bear in mind, " *que c'eft Marc Aurèle qui parle, ce n'eft pas moi:* " it is DON BALTASAR's pen this philippic emanates from, not mine ; and that the *you* and *I* here invoked are himfelf and DON BARTHOLOMEW DE MORLANES. I myfelf—I, gentle reader—have fpared you not only the battering-rams of *italics* with which Don Baltafar affaults this official Growley of *his* day, but even all the CAPITALS (at leaft all thofe of Europe) that he had crammed into this paffage, to make it the more impregnable and impofing.

fault too, that it alienates all civilized people from you, and banifhes them from your houfe and prefence. Have you a mind to recover and bring back thefe amiable fugitives? do but put on a gracious, obliging air; that attraction alone will bring them all again; for that metamorphofis and change of the exterior will perfuade them there was firft of all one within.'

"A volume would not be fufficient to particularize all the advantages of an agreeable manner. It intermixes fo many civil things, even in a refufal, that we fcarcely perceive it to be one. At leaft, we take it more kindly than a favour granted us with an ill grace and reluctant countenance. It fo qualifies a reprimand too, that it makes it appear more like an admonition than a reproof. Under a kind approbation of our conduct, which it feems to look upon as difcreet, it will couch and infinuate a genteel(!) remonftrance, finely to point out and intimate to us, that we are not fo perfect as we fhould be. In a word, Manner is a fort of univerfal fpecific for all diforders,[1] an univerfal fupplement

---

[1] If Don Baltafar be right, *this* quite accounts—defpite our draining and lighting and fanitary improvements—for our ever-increafing bills of mortality; but it's an ill wind (and *not*, it would appear, an ill manner,) that blows nobody any good; and what a paradife England muft be, and *is*, for M.D.s! They have only to make a name, and, like Mofes

to all defects and imperfections, an univerfal means towards an univerfal fuccefs.

"But after all, fay you, what is this manner you fpeak of? in what does it precifely confift? It is, in fhort, a thing not to be defined; for it confifts in a certain *je ne fçay quoi* [*je ne fais quoi*], an indefinable fomething, that cannot be explained either. Without attempting, then, to analyze its nature and effence, I fhall only call it an affemblage, or conjunction of perfections, a mafter-piece of work, finifhed by the hands of all the Graces.

"We need not go back to former ages for an example of this mafterpiece, this inexplicable, in-expreffible, fomething. Ifabella de Bourbon, Queen of Caftile, was poffeffed of this union of perfections, attefted by the general admiration and applaufe of all Spain, not to mention a thoufand other qualities, which gained her more glory than any queen of her name ever merited in this kingdom. This princefs had fuch a charming manner, fuch engaging, winning ways, an affability fo natural, eafy, and yet majeftic, that fhe won the hearts of all who approached her. She did a great deal in a little time. She lived uni-verfally admired, and died univerfally lamented.

---

in the "Vicar of Wakefield," to go to fleep. They need fear no rival healers in good manners!

" Heaven foon claimed this angelic vertue [*i. e.* virtue], of which this world was not worthy. Ifabella de Bourbon, after having been the too fhort-lived felicity of this kingdom, was taken hence to the fruition of an eternal felicity prepared for her merits."

But to return to our own bad manners. I do maintain that they arife more from intenfe felfifhnefs than pride, as foreigners fuppofe ; or rather that pride, the vulgar fungus commonly fo called, is but the fecondary refult of the firft principle, felfifhnefs. As one, among many inftances, of the fort of almoft incredibly bad manners which perfons are fubjected to in this country in their unavoidable public intercourfe with their compatriots, I will relate one of which I was eye and ear witnefs. A fhort time ago, on a fummer's Sabbath evening, I ftrolled into a mediæval church to look at the monuments and painted windows, which during the fervice I had of courfe been unable to examine. I foon perceived that I was not alone in my explorations, but that two ladies—I mean LADIES—were fimilarly employed. At length, tired by their refearches, they entered a pew near the reading defk, while I foon after took poffeffion of an oppofite one. The two ladies upon going into their feat had knelt down to pray, we three being the only perfons then in the church.

They had fcarcely concluded their devotions when the firft bell began to toll for evening prayers, and foon after the verger came down the centre aifle, and after having lit the gas at the reading defk, handed them a hymn book, which feemed to endorfe, as it were, their right to the places they had felected, though no doubt they, like myfelf, were under the impreffion that at the evening fervice, whoever came firft were free to take any vacant feat they chofe. All went on fmoothly till towards the end of the Firft Leffon, when two young—*ladies*, I fuppofe they would have called themfelves—but terribly beflowered, befurbelowed and befeathered figures, came ruftling and buftling down the aifle, and, not fpeaking in that low, fubdued tone which inferiors generally adopt before their earthly fuperiors—ftill more in the Houfe of God— they dafhed open (for I can defcribe it in no other way) the pew door where the two ladies fat, and faid in a *loud* voice, "You can't fit here —this is *our* pew."

Now what confiderably added to the *Chriftian* grace of this proceeding was, that there was ample room in the pew for four. The LADIES did not wait for a fecond notice to quit, and opening my pew door for them I betook myfelf to another, not but what there was plenty of room in the one I occupied; but after the fpecimen of good breeding they had juſt experienced I thought they might prefer being alone.

This accurſed omnipreſence of ſelf is for ever riſing to the ſurface, and tainting and twanging all beneath, like that horrid oil by which the Italians exclude the air (at the expenſe of the flavour of the wine) on the top of their flaſks of Monte Pulciano and Falernian ; or that "*Spirate* of Cinnamon," which Algernon Sidney wrote to his friend, Mr. Furley, at the Hague, to get for him, with the warmeſt Indian gown he could find at Amſterdam, adding, touching the *Spirate :*—

" Perhaps you may at the ſame place *heare* of that ſpirate of cinnamon that you ſent me once into France, and I ſhould be glad to have as much more now, if I could have that which is right and good, but I *heare* there is knavery in *that buſineſſe* as well as many others ; and the way of ſending the laſt, with *Oile* on the top, was good to preſerve it, but I never found a way ſoe to take it off but it mixed with the *ſpirate* and ſpoilt the taſte and ſmell."

And verily ſo does this rancid oil of ſelfiſhneſs (which is intended as a ſafeguard to the body over which it preſides) " mix with the ſpirit," and ſpoil the flavour and aroma of all other qualities. And the worſt effect of this ſelfiſh-neſs is, that the heart, which God made and intended to be *elaſtic*, is hardened and narrowed into a pſychology of the Greek ſculptor's " Homunculus meaſuring the Coloſſal Statue by its Thumb." Theſe ſelfiſh homunculi meaſure all greatneſs by ſome homœopathic rule of thumb of their own. A large heart, a great mind, and ſtill more, a great nature, *they* cannot underſtand; and only look upon them as convenient reſervoirs of folly for ſupplying their wants. So that with ſuch perſons, let them be under whatſoever obligations they may to others, decency is difficult, and gratitude impoſſible. For in every way they are as tough and obtuſe as a rhinoceros; to win them is alſo impoſſible, to offend them is equally ſo; for their own intereſt, or at leaſt *ends*, being the only thing they keep ſteadily in view, though under ordinary circumſtances their manners may be uncouth and repulſive in the extreme, yet no ſooner is it a queſtion of inſult verſus intereſt than ſtraight they are

> " Made all of falſe-faced ſoothing, when ſteel grows
> Soft as the paraſite's ſilk."

And oh! how ſhocked ſuch reptiles are, with their toad-like fibres that can diſpenſe with the very breathing element of other natures, and ſtill drag on their ſlow, cold, marrowleſs exiſtence, how utterly ſcandalized they are, when they have goaded fome frank, honeft nature, by treachery and bafe ingratitude, into one of thofe terrific heart-quakes, where

> " What the breaft forges the tongue muft vent;
> And being angry, do forget that ever
> They heard the name of death."

For then the *fæva indignatio* reigns fupreme.

Well-bred perfons, whatever inconvenience they may put themfelves to or facrifices they may make to ferve another, were it to the amount of more than half their worldly goods, would of courfe *leffen* and make light of the favour to the *obligée;* but towards the genuine Anglo-Saxon this is a moft fupererogatory piece of delicate generofity, as they are fure to put *that* conftruction on it, and to point it out to you, fo as in fact to tranfpofe the pofitions, and endeavour out of your own mouth to prove that *you*, not *they*, are the debtor; for moft perfons, though by no means too proud to accept any fort of affiftance, are generally too mean to acknowledge it. If out of *fheer* compaffion, at a great facrifice of perfonal or pecuniary comfort, you give houfe-lefs and friendlefs perfons a home, though they may be morally and phyfically everything that is moft antipathic and obnoxious to you; when on the firft opportunity they play you fome Judas trick, and you are ftung by their bafe

ingratitude into complaining of the bad return
fuch conduct is for the years of kindnefs they
have received from you, the odds are they
tell you " Why, you yourfelf told me that, fo
folitary a life as you led, it was quite an acquifi-
tion to have any one to ftay with you!" or if,
out of the fame foolifh compaffion, you have
allowed fome thoroughly difagreeable and in no
way defirable perfon to infeft your houfe all the
year round, merely becaufe you knew he or fhe
wanted a dinner, and had not the means of pro-
curing it; and that further, you had adminiftered
to his or her pecuniary neceffities far more largely
than your own warranted—when the turn of the
wheel feparates you, whatever forrows or mif-
fortunes may befall you, though they be not of a
defcription fimilar to thofe you relieved in them,
and though there are pens, ink, paper, and poftal
arrangements all the world over, not one word
of fympathy or remembrance will you receive
from your *friends*, till, perhaps, at the end of
another decade, they may want again a fum of
money; and not knowing any other fool fo likely
as the former oft-tried one to give it them, *then*
will come a letter faying, " from your many
former profeffions of friendfhip, he or fhe is fure
you will not refufe," but not one fyllable about
or allufion to the many fignal fervices they had
received from you; the truth of the matter being

that you never had felt or could feel, for fo narrow and fordid a nature, any friendfhip; ftill lefs had you *profeffed* to do fo, though out of fheer compaffion for their diftrefs you *had done* them many fignal fervices. But the *fuppreffio veri* and *fuggeftio falfi* are infeparable from little minds and fhallow hearts in *all* things, but more efpecially where gratitude is due, and being thoroughly infolvent in that virtue, like other unprincipled creditors, they prefer fwindling you by any dirty quibble or chicanery. Not that I have any pecuniary debtors, for to that fort of perfon I never lend money, but always give it; which is a practical illuftration of making a virtue of neceffity; for as I am very fure it would never be repaid it is as well to take the initiative, and by robbing onefelf fave them the additional fin of defrauding one. Now all this dearth of proper feeling and good principle is difgufting and difcouraging in the extreme; not as regards onefelf individually; for anyone who does a kind act, be it great or fmall, from a motive of praife, reward, or gratitude, or indeed from *any* motive but the ONE golden one enjoined to us from above, of DOING UNTO OTHERS AS WE WOULD THEY SHOULD DO UNTO US, deferves not only ingratitude, but cenfure; but it *is* dif- couraging, when one *hears* fo much about the alchemic power of Progrefs, to find how very,

very little it has yet done towards tranfmuting the drofs of human nature. Perhaps all this arifes from our being in a tranfition ftate, wherein the fine old title of GENTLEMAN is much abufed; indeed, the race of men and women (like that of children) appears to be extinct; *all* perfons are ladies and gentlemen nowadays, which may account for a gentleman or a gentlewoman, in the fingular number, being fo rare. I only wonder that maids-of-all-work don't advertife as *ladies* not objecting to do houfehold work, when a far lower clafs of perfons, thofe figuring in ftreet brawls and police reports, tenacioufly infift upon the grade; for we conftantly read, " the prifoner denied having punched the *lady's* eye or torn her bonnet; he and *another gentleman* were going along, and merely afked her the way to Oxford Street." * * And the other day there was an account of a poor over-driven bull rufhing into a public-houfe, where two builders were drinking and fmoking their pipes in the tap-room; and the public was informed that after fetting all the taps of the fpirit-barrels flowing " in its headlong courfe, the bull rufhed into the tap-room, where the two *gentlemen* were fmoking," &c.

Speaking of bulls naturally reminds one of Irifh labourers, the lower order of which are very witty *gentlemen* indeed, and what is better, have wit in their anger, and when they meet with a *jauntleman* who has no pretenſion to being a gentleman, they know how to repay his ingratitude in his own coin. A happy inſtance of this occurred at a faſhionable watering-place a ſhort time ago. A portly " well-to-do " looking *gentleman* was out boating for his pleaſure in a ſomewhat rough ſea ; a ſudden guſt capſiſed the boat, all hands ſtruck out for the ſhore, but the ſtout gentleman, though accuſtomed to keep his head above water all his life, evidently did not know how to ſwim, and in fact was in imminent danger, when a poor Iriſhman ſtanding on the eſplanade threw off his coat, jumped into the ſea, and at the riſk of his own life ſaved that of the ſtruggling man, and bore him to ſhore amid the loud cheers of the ſpectators. No ſooner did the *gentleman* in broadcloth find himſelf on *terra firma*, and give himſelf a ſort of Newfoundland-doggiſh ſhake in order to make ſure of his own identity, than, putting his hand into his pocket, he generouſly preſented his deliverer with Sixpence ! Pat put it on the palm of his left hand, which he held out at arm's length, and contemplated it in every poſſible light, making the moſt comical face imaginable at it—ſuch as Gulliver may have done at the firſt Liliputian that he ſcrutiniſed in the ſame way—only the Iriſhman ſcratched his head with his right hand the while, till ſuddenly running after the ſtout gentleman, he touched him on the arm with one hand, while between the finger and thumb of the other he tendered him the coin, throwing back his head in a deprecating fort of way, as he faid out loud for every one to hear—

" Here it is, *fur*—I *cudn't, indade* I *cudn't;* it would go *agin me* confcience entirely, to take *fich* a fum from yez ; for faix ! it's *jift* fivepence halfpenny *tree* fardings more *nor* yer worth ! "

If roars of laughter could avenge or reward, Pat was amply compenfated and avenged. But the ftout gentleman was faved for the nonce, and to perfons of an habitual and ftony felfifhnefs[1] it never occurs, when an immediate danger or neceffity is once paft, that difafters and dilemmas at all events are conftantly repeating themfelves ; and that the rinds of the oranges they have fqueezed and are therefore fo prompt to fling away, may under fome other and future phafe of their career be again ufeful to them. For they do not reflect that in this fhort-fighted ingratitude to its agents it is Providence itfelf that they outrage, which may teach them the leffon they fo much require in the fevere fchool of retribution when next fate

---

[1] No doubt fome will exclaim, " But the ftout gentleman's ungrateful conduct arofe from fheer ftinginefs, and not from felfifhnefs or ill breeding." Pardon me, my dear fir or madam ; but if *well* analyfed, you will find that *all* meannefs, but more efpecially pecuniary meannefs, is nothing but the hardeft fort of felfifhnefs, or petrified egotifm.

places a fpringe, a pitfall, or a barrier in their way. Alas! fuch natures but too incontrovertibly prove to us that Martial was not far wrong when he afferted that animals are often more generous than the felf-ftyled "paragon of animals," MAN; for they evince on many occafions a fort of humanity where men fhow nothing but brutality, "and if quadrupeds degenerate fometimes on this fcore," adds the poet, "it is only becaufe they are corrupted by the examples of men."

And fo far he is right, for being all the creatures of habit, we are of neceffity influenced and moulded more by example than by precept; and our intenfe felfifhnefs, and the bad manners and ill breeding growing out of them arife from early mifrule, and being allowed to indulge in them in our own families, and where, defpite the *verbal* moral axioms they *hear* (of which even among the leaft virtuous there is never any lack) they are naturally led to practife what they *fee.* For as Lord Bacon truly obferves in one of his ableft effays, that " *Of Cuftome and Education,*" "Many examples may be put of the force of *Cuftome,* both upon *Minde* and body. Therefore fince *Cuftome* is the *principall* magiftrate of man's life, let men by all means endeavour to obtain good *Cuftomes,* and certainly *Cuftome* is more perfect when it beginneth in young years."

But it is the little *bienséances* and all-buying and little-cofting amenities of fociety, thofe little things of GREAT IMPORT, the minor morals of life, in which, nationally fpeaking, we are fo lamentably deficient, all of which *lèfe-bienféances* might be eafily avoided if we would make it a rule to fay to ourfelves, "If this were a king, a queen, or any other great perfonage, or one from whom I wanted or expected fomething, or that it was in any way my intereft to pleafe or to con-ciliate, would I thus cavalierly keep them waiting, or break an appointment of my own making? or leave their letter unanfwered? or fhow how much their vifit bored or deranged me? or curtly refufe any requeft they might make me? or *ungracioufly* grant it? or be fo inadvertent as to fay or do the very thing which I was perfectly aware was the thing of all others moft calculated to wound or annoy them?" Confcience could have but one anfwer to this catechifm—an unqualified No!

Then believe me it is wrong fo to act towards our uninfluential equals, doubly wrong if there is anything unjuft and exceptional in their pofition or circumftances, which fhould on that account be given by courtefy the higheft rank, and treated with every deference and confideration. And trebly wrong is this ill-bred remiffnefs towards our focial inferiors and dependants. But when we are guilty of any of thefe fhortcomings we fhould take heed that the remedy be not worfe than the difeafe—that is, that the apology, from an affumption of patronage and implied fuperiority, be not more offenfive than the original rudenefs. For here again our national *gaucherie* and omniprefence of felf generally tranfpofes the pofitions, and inftead of expreffing (as common good breeding demands) *their* regret and lofs at not having been able to come and fee you for fo long a time, they generally begin by condoling with *you*, for *your* difappointment in not having feen them, and fearing you muft have thought them very unkind. But the worft of thefe epidemic bad manners is that they are infectious, for it is not in human nature, if too long goaded, to refift the temptation of retaliation, as, like all other animals of better inftincts and lefs reafon, we are apt under great provocation to confound retaliation with redrefs, and fo, for the moft part, follow the example of the King of Bavaria, who faid, when Napoleon I. kept him and feveral other legitimate royalties waiting for him for a full hour of a bitter cold January day in the carriage at the gates of Malmaifon while he was paying a *fub rofâ* vifit to his divorced Jofephine: "Puifqu'on nous traite comme des laquais, ma foi! divertons-nous comme tels;"[1]—and forthwith difpatched a real lackey to a neighbouring *cabaret* for bread, cheefe, and wine.

In footh, all bad manners and vulgar reprifals *have* a fpice of the lackey in them.

---

[1] "Since we are treated like footmen, the beft thing we can do is to amufe ourfelves in the fame way as if we really were Knights of the Shoulder-Knot."

SAMUEL PEPYS AND FRANCIS BACON, LORD VERULAM AND VISCOUNT ST. ALBANS.

AMUEL PEPYS and Lord Bacon : one of the ' *littleſt* ' and one of the greateſt men who ever lived ! " Why, what a jumble !" exclaims the reader, " for even chronologically ſpeaking, Lord Bacon ought to have precedence."

> " True, I grant you, on that ground alone,
> But on none other, as it ſhall be ſhown."

This, the nineteenth century, among many more high-ſounding titles, calls itſelf an age of pro-greſs, but *that* it never can or will be ſo long as mere intellectual ſupremacy continues to paſs current for an all-ſufficient expiation of every ſpecies of moral obliquity and turpitude. Therefore ſhall Francis Lord Bacon, " the brighteſt, wiſeſt, meaneſt of mankind," be weighed in the balance with Samuel Pepys, and be found wanting. Sylla wifely chofe the title of *Felix* rather than that of *Magnus;* we do the very reverfe. The whole ftudy of the age is to be great—not in reality, for that were meritorious, but in appearance; for this is effentially an era of fhams and feemings. However, deduced from the falfe premifes from which we ftart in all things, this is · fo far logical, that we *may* be apparently great upon falfe pretences; whereas, in order to be happy, we muft return to firft principles, thofe that we fet before the children in their copy-books; that is, we muft be GOOD. Don't be alarmed; I am not going to give you an elaborate differtation, reader, upon that un-known pagan divinity, fuppofed to be VIRTUE, but as to whofe nomenclature no two heathens, however illuftrious, could ever agree, Ariftotle calling it the glory of humanity; Salluft, the badge of immortality; Seneca, man's only good; Cicero, the root of happinefs; Apuleius, the imprefs of the Deity; Sophocles, inexpreffible riches; Euripides, a rare treafure; Virgil, the beauty of the foul; Cato, the foundation of authority; Socrates, the fountain of felicity; Menander, his buckler; Horace, his ftrength; Bias, his all; Valerius Maximus, a thing inef-timable; Plautus, the price of all things; Cæfar, the perfection of all great qualities; and which, in the eighteenth century, under the auspices of Mr. Samuel Richardson, culminated in "Pamela," and was for the firft and laft time REWARDED!

No, no! if my betters could not break in this Cruifer of an attribute, fo as that "a child might ride it," I am not going to attempt it. Why fhould I, when Socrates, who had the advantage of living in an age and country where there was no law of libel, and no periodical prefs nor Quarterly Reviews, gave it as his opinion that there was not a man living who thoroughly underftood anything? If this was the cafe *then*, when there was fo much lefs to *be* underftood, and fo many more people to underftand it, (philofophers included), what Bœotian imbecility it would be in me, who am a lineal defcendant from Socrates' majority (limited), to attempt to analyfe the problematic concrete! I only meant to fay, and I repeat it, that in order to be happy we muft be good, and in this at once fimple yet profound art, Heaven itfelf has condefcended to be our teacher; for unto every foul born into this world God has given a moral chronometer, called confcience, which He has originally fet by his own great horologe of omnifcience and eternity; if we neglect it, it will run down and be filent; if we tamper with it, and regulate it according to falfe computations, it will deceive both ourfelves and others; but it cannot deceive the Maker, who knows that all its works were perfect when it left His hands; and will demand a ftrict account of the manner in which they have been neglected or perverted.

For which reafon, I fhall proceed to prove that the little, pompous, whilom Secretary of the Admiralty, Samuel Pepys, was, not a better, but certainly *a lefs bad* man than Francis Lord Bacon, Lord High Chancellor of England; *both* having (with fome exceptions, greatly in favour of Pepys) the fame range of vices in perfection. For though a brother chancellor might find that "there was not fo much amifs in my Lord Verulam"[1]—probably becaufe in this age of mouth amenity and moral turpitude, it is part of the *arcana cana* of our fyftem of popular fallacies to confider it *contra bonos mores* to breathe a *word* againft a predeceffor (however remote), or indeed

---

[1] All Mr. Hepworth Dixon's apotheofis of Lord Bacon (publifhed fince this was written) goes to prove is, that bribery, corruption, and felf-feeking were more openly and honeftly carried on in thofe days than they are now, and that my Lord Verulam was no worfe than his contemporaries— only managed ugly bufineffes more cleverly. The worft thing againft him is the *primâ facie* evidence; for it is a villainous countenance, fuch a one as Lavater would have paffed the fame fentence upon that he did on Mirabeau: "You have every vice, and have done nothing to check them."

to fpeak the truth about any one, or any thing, if it can be poffibly avoided—yet any graduate of a ragged fchool well up in his Catechifm and the Ten Commandments would be inclined to hold a different opinion of my Lord Bacon. Of courfe, no one cognizant of the economy, not to fay parfimony of Nature, in the production of real greatnefs and fuperiority, whether in the moral, animal, vegetable, or mineral kingdoms, is fo unreafonable as to expect that John Bramftones fhould grow upon every bramble—that righteous judge of Charles I.'s time, whom hiftorians concur in telling us " popularity could never flatter into anything unfafe, nor favour bribe to anything unjuft," ftill there are degrees in everything, and there is, moreover, fuch a thing as wearing one's vices, like one's rue, " with a difference."

Having given Mr. Pepys the *pas* in the firft inftance, I fhall continue to do fo, making a little hieroglyphical fum in addition (as he himfelf might have done) of his merits and demerits and thofe of Lord Bacon ; fetting down 1 whenever the balance is in favour of the Secretary, and o when it is againft the Chancellor.

Pepys.

Pepys kept a Diary or Confeffional, and open confeffion is good for the foul.

In that diary, with unexampled candour, and to fave that celeftial fecretary, the recording angel, trouble at the Day of Judgment, he pithily gives his motives for refufing a tempting bribe that had been offered him to do a little dirty work.

"For I did not think them fafe men to receive fuch a gratuity from, and that I might have it in my power to fay I *had* refufed it."

The mean, felfifh motives for this right conduct are fhared by thoufands of highly refpectable individuals. The unflinching honefty of voluntarily acknowledging them is perhaps UNIQUE.

Pepys, as we have feen, did not take bribes; and inftead of hypocritically anathematizing all who were guilty of that iniquity, he honeftly, if not exactly nobly (!) tells us *why* he did not do fo; at all events, he avoided the committal of the fin, though neither purity nor principle had anything to do with his integrity. But on the very rare occafions that cowardice makes men act honeftly, it is hard that the trembling monitor fhould not receive its meed of praife. Neither did Pepys delude and betray his fuitors. On the contrary, he fpent much time in figning pardons gratis, as was proved by the following

Bacon.

Lord Bacon did not. *He* was wiſer (in his generation), and wrote pompous eſſays denunciatory of his own eſpecial vices.

My Lord Verulam invariably took bribes with *both* hands — that is, from his client and his client's adverſary—and whichever bribe weighed the heavieſt furniſhed him with the moſt weighty reaſons for *legally* deciding in favour of the donor. Yet hear how this intellectual Janus, this judicial Judas, *wrote* upon this very iniquity of bribery :—

*   *   *   *   *

" The Vices of *Authority* are chiefly *foure :—Delaies ; Corruption ; Roughneſs ; and Facilitie.* For *Delaies* give eaſie acceſſe; keepe times appointed. Go through with that that is in hand ; and interlace not buſineſſe, but of neceſſity. For *Corruption ; Do not only bind thine own hands from taking, but alſo thy ſervants' hands from taking, but bind the hands of ſutours* [*ſuitors*] *alſo from offering* [!] *For integrity uſed doth the one ; but integrity profeſſed, and with a manifeſt deteſtation of* BRIBERY [!!] *doth the other. And avoid not only the fault, but the ſuſpicion.*" !!!

(As my Lord Bacon evidently thought he was cleverly doing by this impious hypocriſy!)

Brought
over
2

PEPYS.

comment in his " Diary " on this philanthropic expenditure of his time : " I got nothing for it, which did trouble me much." *Anglicè*, like many more, he had much trouble for nothing. *Poverino* Pepys !

THE TWO CLOAKS.

Pepys alfo combined loyalty with economy, and if he often evinced the fpirit of his father the tailor, he invariably efchewed the *goofe*, where his own pocket and perfon were concerned. So the Diary has the following very fenfible entry, which was no doubt the aboriginal "COMBINING ELEGANCE WITH ECONOMY" now fo common in tailors' advertifements :—

" I did countermand the making of my velvet cloak for a time, till I fhould fee which way the queen's illnefs did iffue."

(Mem.) Pepys had never received any honours or emoluments from Charles II.'s queen, as Lord Bacon had done from Elizabeth.

Pepys, on the contrary, never betrayed or did anything to injure *his* patrons, my Lord Sandwich or the king; but on the contrary, was remarkably civil and *prévenant* always to their refpective "Miffes," as honorary wives were in thofe days called. And upon once being preffed

BACON.

" *Whofoever is found Variable, and changeth manifeftly, without manifeft caufe, giveth fufpicion of Corruption.*"

(For which reafon my Lord Verulam never *changed*, for he never *decided* till he knew he had good and *fufficient* reafons for his decifion.)

IN HYPOCRISY FIVE HUNDRED FATHOMS BELOW PEPYS.

OOOOO

THE TWO CLOAKS.

When on the 23rd of March, 1602, the day before Queen Elizabeth died, my Lord Verulam took water at Whitehall to go down to Richmond " to inquire how long the Queene's Highneffe was like to laft, he chid his ferving man for giving him his beft cloake,—when neither the queene, nor the weather, were like to hold out. On getting to Richmond he met Dr. Whitgift, the Archbifhop of Canterbury, who told him the Queene had juft commanded her coronation ring, which had grown into the flefh, to be filed off her finger : and the almonds of her ears having begun to fwell and an univerfal numbnefs to feize her. She was far on her laft journey. The rain now beginning to come down, my Lord hafted back to his barge, well pleafed that he had had more forethought than his

Brought
over
4

PEPYS.

to cook certain accounts he flatly refufed, as the Diary tells us, " from fear, and from unwillingnefs to wrong the king; and *becaufe it was no profit to me* " [!] Here is Truth again, in her anti-crinoline coftume, drawn up out of her well, and the parifh beadle and county gaol on active fervice, *vice* confcience and honour, promoted. Then Pepys, though he was always making effays on love, never wrote one; and whether we contemplate him being fpat upon at " the play-houfe " by a lady, and not minding it when he found fhe was pretty, or getting up an ecftafy at the fight of Lady Caftlemaine's " *laced fmock as it did hang out to dry,*" or giving "Nym" £5, when he only gave Mrs. P— £2, as will fome-times happen in the beft regulated families, he was always the greateft gallant poffible in a fmall way.

I

    Pepys carried always about him in his beft coat pocket, and did not care to fhare its con-tents with any one fo long as it contributed to his own perfonal comfort, a fmall homœopathic cafe of poifonous globules of the moft infinitefimal variety, which he took regularly and felt quite comfortable, even to thinking when he was in his own beft Niagara of a wig, with its cataracts of curls, that in *défhabille* the king was but a poor

BACON.

<table>
<tr><td>

fervitors, not to wafte *a faire cloake on foule weather!*"

My Lord Verulam, having too great a mind for fo lowly and humble a virtue as gratitude to take root in, *prudently* betrayed his too generous friend, patron, and benefactor, Effex, thinking, no doubt, that for a genius with fuch a head as his, a friend's head was as good a ftepping-ftone as any in the court of fo profligate, heartlefs, and un-womanly a fovereign as Elizabeth. What a pity it is that he did not *leave to the world, and after a while to this country,* an effay on Gratitude as well as that on "Love!" as it would, there is little doubt, have been well worthy of the man who wrote : " It is a poor faying of Epictetus— *Satis magnum alter, alteri theatrum fumus*—as if a man, made for the contemplation of Heaven and all noble objects had nothing to do but kneel before a little Idoll and make himfelfe fub-ject, though not of the mouth (as Beafts are), yet of the eye, which is given for higher purpofes !"

Lord Bacon's felf-valuation was allopathic and coloffal, and he purpofely bequeathed it to the world as an all-fufficient portion. The ftu-pendous brilliancy of fuch an intellect, in the midft of fo low and miry a moral organization, may be compared to a Bude light in a charnel

</td><td>

Brought
over
OOOOOO
O

O

O

</td></tr>
</table>

Brought
over
5

Pepys.

looking fellow, though when filked and fatined he looked noble. Pepys, with all his little Liliputian pompofity, never hypocritically pointed out the right way to others; he only took care to go by it himfelf, *not* from the glorious immortality pro-mifed at the end of it—for he had no fuch lofty afpirings — but becaufe he dreaded the fnares, fpring guns, and foul things that might bemire his fine clothes, or even the cafualties that might ftrip him of them altogether, if, tempted by a fhort cut, he took a wrong turn.

6

BACON.

houſe, illuminating in all its loathſomeneſs the corruption it could not purify.   He *knew* what was right, and pointed it out to others, not indeed from a laudable wiſh for their welfare, but to put them by hypocriſy on a wrong ſcent ; and while indicating to them the beſt road, prevent their perceiving the crooked and foul ways by which he himſelf travelled.[1]

---

[1] But all this is only a proof how well my Lord Verulam underſtood and pra&ctiſed his own axioms on "*vaine glory*," which are ſo perfe&ctly underſtood and carried out alſo in our own times.   "In fame of learning," ſaith he, "the flight will be ſlow without ſome feathers of *Oſtentation. Qui de contemnendâ Gloriâ libros ſcribunt, Nomen ſuum inſcribunt.* SOCRATES, ARISTOTLE, GALEN, were men full of *oſtentation.* Certainly *vaine glory* helpeth to perpetuate a man's memory ; and Vertue was never ſo beholding to Humane Nature, as it received its due at the ſecond hand.   Neither had the Fame of *Cicero, Seneca, Plinius Secundus,* borne her age ſo well, if it had not bin joined with ſome *vanity* in themſelves.   Like unto varniſh, that maketh feelings [ceilings] not only to ſhine, but laſt."   All of which, though elaborately pra&ctiſed now, was condenſed in the Syrian proverb ſome thouſands of years ago, "Give yourſelf *one* ear-ring of gold, and the world will ſoon give you the other."

Having now fhown, what Lord Bacon himfelf would have called "A TABLE OF THE COLOURS OR APPEARANCES OF GOOD AND EVILL, AND THEIR DEGREES, AS PLACES OF PERSWASSION AND DISWASION, AND THEIR SEVERAL FALLAXES AND THE ELENCHES OF THEM," between the pigmy and the giant, it is clearly proved, by moral gauge, which is God's meafure and the only one we fhall be judged by hereafter, although it is quite the reverfe *here*, that although with regard to their fmall vices it is fix of one and half-a-dozen of the other, between the Chancellor and the fecretary, yet morally fpeaking the balance is in favour of the latter; Samuel Pepys being on the *fame* fcores fix times a lefs bad man than FRANCIS LORD BACON. The how, when, and wherefore, of this great famenefs, yet great difference, in the *modus operandi* of fimilar vices in two individuals created out of fuch widely different argils and in antipodical fpiritual and intellectual hemifpheres, muft be left to metaphyficians to determine.

Dr. Clarke and Wollafton confidered moral obligation as arifing from the effential difference and relations of things; Shaftefbury and Hutchefon as arifing from the moral fenfe; and the generality of divines as arifing folely from the will of God. On thefe three principles practical morality has been built. "Thus has God been pleafed," adds Warburton, "to give three different excitements to the practife of virtue, that men of all ranks, conftitutions, and educations might find their account in one or other of them,—something that would hit their palate, fatisfy their reafon, or fubdue their will. But this admirable provifion for the fupport of virtue hath been in fome meafure defeated by its pretended advocates, who have facrilegioufly untwifted this threefold cord."

Exactly fo, and this brings us to the great and infoluble problem of why it fo often happens that the cleareft and loftieft intellects, as in the inftance of Lord Bacon, are found linked with the very bafeft moral obliquities. This, truly, is the Mezentian punifhment, of the dead body bound and chained to the living one, fpiritualized, and perpetuated on into an inexorable eternity. Such men, who have for the moft part but a fmall *worldly* ambition, even to achieve *that* play the wrong card; for nothing in heaven or earth has any vitality in it fave *goodnefs—not* the *appearance* but the REALITY.

If God Himfelf were merely great it is very probable that we fhould even be *afraid* to pray to Him; Omnipotence may will, and in willing awe; Omnifcience may know, and with the fubtle myfteries of fuch infinite knowledge work miracles; but it is GOODNESS alone which can fave or attract, for Goodnefs is the heart of Time and the foul of Eternity. When we appeal to God it is *not* His power we invoke; on the contrary, we often dread that; but it is to his GOODNESS we pray, and to *that* we TRUST.

If the *manes* of the departed are cognizant of the phantafmagoria going on in this world after they have paffed the great Rubicon, and ftill more, if they can either gladden or wince under the pofthumous verdicts of their fellow men, I cannot imagine my Lord Verulam's punifh-ment having reached its grand climacteric, or his myriads of defrauded clients being appeafed, till he found himfelf coupled with Samuel Pepys, and even lofing by the comparifon!

Notwithftanding this *Fiat juftitia*, however, I feel bound to return my grateful thanks for the many pleafant hours I have paffed with my Lord Bacon, more efpecially in his "Gardens," wondering the while when he talked fo much of DEW-BAYES yielding fuch fweet odours of a morning, "GERMANDERS,[1] that give fuch good flower to the eye," with "CORNELIANS," and

---

[1] Doubtlefs the "PRIME-ROSES" mentioned fo often, and with befitting praifes, by Lord Bacon, were merely the an-ceftors of our own little darling meadow-ftars the Primrofes; and, like all other names, theirs was originally beftowed to defignate a peculiarity or a quality, that of their being the firft rofes of the year.

for fruits, of " Ginnitings," " Quadlings,"
and " Melo-Cotones "—I could not help wondering, I fay, the while, what and where they
were; though I could perceptibly inhale the perfume of the dainty mufk-rofes, that of the woo-
ing white violets, and the fpicy tufted pinks,
in all directions.

For the benefit of a certain clafs of young
ladies who may not have read his " Effaies," from
thinking Bacon vulgar in any fhape, I will leave
the "Gardens" and return into the " Buildings,"
and go into that " *Goodly Roome above ftaires of fome
forty feet high,*" or rather into the fmall *fanctum*
next to it, on "*the houfehold fide,*" and take from
under a heap of parchments that little fquare
booke with its red edges, bearing date 1597, being
the firft edition of thofe wonderful " Effaies," and
read you one of the quainteft, that "Of Masques
and Triumphs," (xxxvii.)—merely afking by
the way, what would be thought of a Lord
Chancellor in the year of grace 1876, who wrote
upon operas and ballets, merely becaufe the
Queen *would* have fuch gauds, and being the
keeper of her Majefty's confcience he thought it
his duty to look after the *coryphées ?*

Of Masques and Triumphs.

THESE things are but Toyes, to come amongſt ſuch ſerious obſervations, but yet, ſince Princes will have ſuch things, it is better they ſhould be Graced with Elegancy, than Daubed with coſt.—*Dancing to Song,* is a thing of great State, and Pleaſure. I underſtand it, that the ſong be in Quire[1] placed aloft, and accompanied with ſome broken Muſicke: And the Ditty fitted to the Divice. *Acting in Song,* eſpecially in *Dialogues,* hath an extreme Good Grace: I ſay *Acting,* not *Dancing :* (for that is a mean, and vulgar Thing ;) And the *Voyces* of the *Dialogue* ſhould be ſtrong and manly (a Baſe, and a Tenour, no Trebble) And the *Ditty* High, and Tragicall ; Not nice, or Dainty. *Severall quires,* placed one over againſt another, and taking the voyce by Catches, *Antheme* wiſe, give great Pleaſure. *Turning dances* into *figure,* is a childiſh Curioſity.—And generally let it be noted, that thoſe Things, which I here ſet downe, are ſuch as do naturally take the ſenſe, and not reſpect petty wonderments. It is true the alterations of ſcenes, abound with *Light,* ſpecially coloured, and varied : And let the Maſquers, or any other, that are to

---

[1] Choir.

come downe from the Scene, have some Motions upon the *Scene* itselfe, before their Comming downe, For it drawes the Eye strangely, and makes it with great pleasure, to see, that, it cannot perfectly discern.—Let the *Songs* be *Loud* and Cheerefull, and not *Chirpings*, and *Pulings*. Let the *Musicke* likewise be *Sharpe* and loud (!) and well placed. The *Colours* that shew best by Candle light, are ; White, Carnation, and a kinde of Seawater-Greene ; and *Ols*, or Spangs,[1] as they are of no great cost, so they are of most Glory [!] ; as for rich *Embroidery*, it is lost and not Discerned. Let the *Sutes* of the Masquers be Gracefull, and such as become the person, when the Vizars are off. Not after examples of known attires ; Turkes, Souldiers, Mariners, and the like. Let *Antimasques* not be long ; they have been commonly of Fooles, Satyres, Baboons, Wilde-Men, Antiques, Beasts, Spirits, Witches, Ethiopes, Pigmies, Turquets [?], Nimphs, Rusticks, Cupids, Statuas, Moving, and the like. As for Angels,—it is not comicall enough [!] to put them in *Anti-masques*, and any thing that is hideous, as Devils, Giants, is on the other side, as unfit : But chiefly let the *Musicke* of them be Recreative, and with some strange changes. Some *Sweet Odours* suddenly coming forth, without any drops falling, are in

---

[1] *i.e.* Oripeaux and spangles.

E

such a Company, as there is Steame and Heat, Things of great Pleasure, and Refreshment. *Double Masques*, one of them, another of Ladies, addeth State and Variety. But all is nothing, except the *Roome* he kept Cleare, and Neat. For *Justs*, *Turneys*,[1] and *Barriers*; the Glories of them are chiefly in the Chariots, wherein the Challengers make their Entry; especially if they be drawne with Strange Beasts; as Lions, Bears, Camels, and the like; or in the Devices of their Entrance, or in Bravery of their Liveries; or in the Goodly Furniture of their Horses, and Armour. But enough of these Toyes."

I think so too; but *Cede magnis !*

---

[1] *i.e.,* Jousts and tourneys.

FORGIVE AND FORGET.

HOEVER firſt linked they twain to-
gether in " holy matrimony " knew
human nature *well;* as forgetting is
the ſynonyme of forgiving. Till we
do forget we cannot forgive. It muſt be an
unchriſtian ſpirit indeed that would not forgive
even the moſt irremediable injuries, *if aſked to do
ſo,* coupled with an aſſurance of ſincere regret, on
the part of the aggreſſor. But there are ſome
natures ſo Phariſaical and mean, that their *modus
operandi* is always to merge a leſſer outrage in a
greater. This is ſheer folly, ſo far as the attempts
at impunity of ſuch evil-doers are concerned ; for
there can be no ſuch thing as willing martyrs
where the faggot and the fire are *alone* provided
and the crown is withheld ;—as to appeal to a
perſon's generoſity is one thing (and with generous natures, to appeal to it is to obtain it), but
to ſwindle them out of it by ſnares and ſubterfuges

is another, and the sure way to render oblivion impossible. For would God Himself forgive us, if, instead of asking His forgiveness in a humble and contrite spirit, we on the contrary tried to shift all the onus of our sins upon Him, saying that if HE had not created us or put temptation in our way we should not have transgressed; and that therefore He must clearly perceive, that he owed *us* great reparation, for having allowed our sins to find us out, and bear the bitter fruit of punishment which we ourselves had planted. And yet there are many such inverse natures, so warped by false pride and low cunning, that they invariably transpose the positions, and arraign their victims for the peril *they* have entailed upon them, whenever detection follows crime; which is precisely the same species of inverted logic resorted to by a certain highwayman in George the First's time; who, upon finding himself for the second time in the dock at the Old Bailey, put his arms akimbo, and knitting his brows and looking the judge full in the face, said in a loud bullying voice, so that the whole court might hear it.—

"Harkee, my lord! *this* is the second time I have stood in this dock; if I find myself here a *third* time I shall bind you over to keep the peace, swearing you have put me three times in fear of my life."

But so indispensable is this Lethean process to forgiveness that with the ungratefully treacherous or the criminally weak, who yield to or connive at the misdeeds of others, against their own better natures, we often find,—that it is part of the inscrutable subtlety of God's chemistry of retribution that *they cannot forget*, and consequently *cannot forgive themselves.* Thus Judas flung down the thirty pieces of silver, and went out and hanged himself, thereby acting as his own judge and executioner. And Suetonius mentions that shortly after the Crucifixion, Tiberius deprived Pontius Pilate of his office, and the ex-procurator retired to Vienna;[1] where, falling into a profound melancholy, he committed suicide.

While then forgiveness of injuries depends so entirely upon the oblivion of them, there are some injuries so chronic, concrete, and ubiquitous, that they are incorporated with not only every SOURCE but with every CHANNEL of our existence, and therefore we must forget *it*, before we can forgive *them.* Moreover, it is an incontrovertible truth, that " Pardon to the injured doth belong ;" therefor is it that evil-doers, that is, aggressors, are always so implacably irate at their victims, putting their deeds into words, and inveigh amain against that English

---

[1] Vienne, in Gaul (France).

focial, literary, and political Bogie—their " ftrong language," while the poor victims can but retort, with Electra in the iambics of Sophocles,

" *You* do the deeds, and your unholy deeds find *me* the words."

What then is to be done, fince oblivion is the only feed from which forgivenefs can fpring, but one thing : pray to God, to give us that forgetful-nefs which will enable us, not merely in words, but in truth and in fpirit, to forgive thofe who have chronically and irreparably injured us? And oh! what a bleffed anchor is it, in life's moft devaftating ftorms, to the beft as well as to the worft amongft us, to remember that even that great omnipotent God of Mercy was once alfo A MAN OF SORROW !

PITY.

T would appear from the following paragraph, which I read the other day in a newfpaper, and indeed from feveral other little inftances that one meets with in life, that Pity—that gentle dew of human kindnefs, which frefhens and fertilifes all upon which it refts,—like money, generally goes to thofe who don't deferve it. Take the following example :—

"There are in Egypt three hundred miles of railroad. When the running of the trains was commenced MUMMIES were ufed for fuel, and are faid to make a very hot fire. The fupply is almoft inexhauftible, and they are ufed by the cord. What a deftiny !"

What a deftiny indeed! For if the mummies retain a *fpice* of fentiment, if it has not been all *pitched* out of them by time, tombs, pyramids, pedantry, and one thing or another, they muſt be charmed to find themſelves not only ſuddenly called upon to be uſeful to other *ſleepers*, whom they never dreamt of, but alſo to think that

"Still in their aſhes glow their wonted fires."

But Pity being the theme, ſhe really might beſtow a tear to think how inanimate, inſentient things, ever outlaſt, in this little material planet of ours, the living, breathing, high-aſpiring heirs of immortality, whoſe vaſſals and gauds they are for a brief ſpace. I have been led to this reflection by the revelations of Egypt, which are likely to beat M. de Cuſtine's "Revelations of Ruſſia" quite out of the field. Monſieur de Mariette, another Frenchman, has diſcovered in one of the tombs of the Egyptian kings the jewel-box of one of Egypt's queens, which, with its contents, is now the admiration of elegant and artistic Paris, where even Oberon's and Titania's choiceſt marts for *bijouterie* and knick-knackery have long been eſtabliſhed, and where the ſhades of Benvenuto Cellini and Aſcanio might revel as in a bright little Elyſium of their own. Well, even *there* is this Egyptian caſket, with its carcanets, creating boundleſs admiration from their elaborate workmanſhip and exquiſite finiſh, which the perfectioniſed art of the preſent day could not ſurpaſs, either in deſign or execution.

Among other things is a small regal crown, cu-
riously wrought in fine gold, and a thick gold
chain six feet long!   Think of *that*, ye alder-
men of England, who eat turtle and green peas!
think of it, I say, *even* if, as the French dra-
matist so sublimely and historically expresses it,
there *does*

   "*Coule dans vos veines le plus* NOBLE *sang d'Angleterre,*"
Et que
   "*Votre bisaïeul a été même* DEUX *fois Lord Maire!*"

In this Egyptian queen's jewel-box there is no
mention made of any large pearls (or " unions,"
as they used to be called,) being found. Perhaps
Cleopatra dissolved the last?   For in Egypt and
in those barbaric times such matters might have
been considered regal luxuries, but in England,
in this enlightened age, when everything is for
the million, unions are dissolved in vinegar daily,
or permanently, as the case may be, by the
Divorce Court, which enacts, not exactly the
Antony, but the antidote, on such occasions.

But though there were no pearls in the casket,
there was a token of that other priceless pearl in
life's bitter cup—LOVE! which, until it *is* dissolved, converts the very bitterest into nectar.
For there was amid this treasure-trove a beau-
tifully chiselled gold plate or medallion, with a
man's portrait upon it, it is supposed, the portrait
of the king, or at all events of the monarch of

its quondam owner's affections, and this, the fragile trinket of fome gala hour, is now all that remains of the imperial archives of that queenly heart, the only veftige of that great world of love it then reigned over. And yet—no; tranfition is *not* death. All other paffions may be mortal, and to be returned to the King of kings at our demife, as the infignia of various orders of knighthood are returned to earthly fovereigns, to be beftowed upon others who fucceed us. But Love is the nucleus of eternity, *the* fubtle all-pervading fluid of that myfterious concrete of immortality of which each human portion is a Soul.

It may, nay, it *muft* change, but it *cannot* die. The light of heaven, the breath of flowers, the fong of birds, the fummer air, the fmile of hope, the figh of memory, are each and all full to over-flowing of it. We fee it, hear it, breathe it, in all things; whether it be in ftorm or in funfhine, in pleafure or in pain, it is *ftill there,*—omniprefent, for it is the atmofphere of God's creation; and who can fay then that the Egyptian queen may not even now be SITTING IN CASSIOPEA'S CHAIR, LOOKING THROUGH A MYRIAD STARRY EYES STILL FONDLY DOWN UPON HER CHERISHED LOVE GIFTS OF LONG LONG AGO!

ON THE GRATITUDE WE OWE
OUR ENEMIES.

T was a pithy ſaying that of Lorenzo de' Medici, and true as pithy, that we are enjoined to forgive our enemies, but nowhere are we told that we ſhould forgive our friends. One thing is certain, that even our moſt inveterate and moſt influential enemies could prevail but little againſt us (ſo invariably does unſcrupulous malice defeat itſelf), but for the treachery, colluſion, cowardice, weakneſs, or imbecility of our nominal friends! Therefore we owe this debt of gratitude to our enemies (and it is not a ſmall one), that they have been the means of our diſcovering the vipers that we have unconſciouſly been warming at our hearths, or worſe ſtill, it may be, in our boſoms, before they had the power of injuring us further. Appeal to any one's experience, and he will tell you that he has largely (that is, with ſo few exceptions as

to eſtabliſh the rule), proved the truth of Rochefoucault's maxim, " Faire un bienfait, faire un ingrat ;" and yet, as in the vegetable and mineral kingdoms there grows an antidote near every poiſon, ſo in the moral world are there innumerable antidotes to this moſt deadly of all poiſons, ingratitude, even in the immenſity of unſuſpected, gratuitous, unalloyed, and therefore almoſt ſublime goodneſs, that exiſts up and down and round about the world. For ſeldom does any flagrant inſtance of baſeneſs or ingratitude befall us, but the reaction of the blow ſtrikes at other hearts that we ignored till then, and ſets the unſealed fountains of their ſympathy and ſenſe of outraged juſtice guſhing towards us in a thouſand acts of kindneſs and devotion. For no tittle of God's word ever fails, and thus is His promiſe fulfilled, that if we caſt our bread upon the waters, after many days it ſhall return to us. But to convince us of our own weakneſs and His ſtrength, it generally does return to us at times and places where we could have leaſt hoped for it, or rather where we moſt deſpaired of it. When the neceſſity is at the greateſt and the ſpirit at the fainteſt, *then* comes the miraculous bread in the wilderneſs, WHICH, OUT OF HUMAN IMPOSSIBILITIES, NOT ONLY SUPPLIES OUR WANTS, BUT EXCEEDS THEM.

A CURIOSITY OF LITERATURE NOT MENTIONED BY ISAAC D'ISRAELI.

THERE are few more charming books in the language for a firefide companion than D'Ifraeli's " Curiofities of Literature." Still a man cannot read everything, any more than he can know everything. And moreover, thofe cocks of the walk in literature may be the very antipodes of the chanticleer celebrated by Æfop. *They* may *only* care for gems, and defpife grains of barley, whereas fortunately for you, friend reader, I'm not proud, and therefore much more refemble the other feathered agriculturift in the fable, from infinitely preferring (where a good laugh is the defideratum) a barley grain, a rogue in grain, or in fhort anything, to a gem; for there is a brilliancy and intrinfic value about all gems which preclude the poffibility of laughing at them. But before I hofpitably and generoufly invite you to fharewith me, dear reader, the particular and somewhat curious grain of barley upon which I happen to be feasting at this time, I'll tell you exactly where I was fortunate enough to scratch it up. Premising that in consequence of the present democratic movement and tendency to fusion of classes, I don't see why asses should not be occasionally stall-fed, poor things! as well as oxen, and therefore, I own it, *I* for one, am much addicted to old book stalls. Shallow people, that is, most persons, often express their wonder, that sleek, civilized, gentlemanlike, well bred, well fed dogs, should be so fond of poking about, and excavating from ineffable garbage all sorts of old bones and fragments in their walks; aye, and even little pampered, petted, affected, fine lady, silken-pawed, velvet-eared Blenheims and King Charleses, have to a speckle, the same *canimania;* but never (though blest with a tolerable good library at home) do I find myself before a stall covered with old dog-eared, dilapidated looking books,—some with shining, dark, gingerbread-looking covers, others in old embossed gold-paper ones, others in parchment that had once been white, till done brown by that swindler, Time, but looking dropsical withal, as if from too deep potations at the Pierian spring, and others with no covers at all,[1]—that I do not perfectly

---

[1] In one of my stall *bones,* to wit, "A Dissertation on

underſtand the phyſiology (perhaps I ought to ſay the philomathy) of the whole affair. For in wiſt-fully eyeing theſe old bones of literature I feel, with the dogs, that what others once feaſted upon may perchance ſtill contain ſome ſcraps worthy either of a dog's noſe or a man's notice ; though both in the canine and the critical reſearch, it cannot be denied that there intermingles a great deal of Dr. Johnſon's definition of a ſecond mar-riage,—namely, " The triumph of hope over ex-perience." However, the identical grain of bar-ley that we are now about to diſcuſs was not ſo much ſought out by me as that it fell in my way. For in a box of books I received lately was a cata-logue of old and ſecond-hand volumes ; in ſpelling

READING THE CLASSICS, and Forming a Juſt Style : addreſſed to The Right Honourable JOHN LORD Roos, the Preſent DUKE OF RUTLAND. By HENRY FELTON, D.D. Printed by Jonah Bowyer, at The Roſe, in St. Paul's Church Yard, 1723," is the following inſtruction to *book keepers, printed* in a ſquare black frame, under the armorial bearings of its former owner, one Mr. Chriſtopher Toogood, and for *this* " Caution to Sinners" it was I bought the volume :—

The firſt thing you ought to do, when you borrow a Book, is, to read it; that you may *return* it as ſoon as poſſible TO THE OWNER.

it over, I was irrefiftibly attracted by the title of the one I am about to lay before you, *not in extenfo*, for *that* would be no joke, but a heavy infliction. And when I received this precious volume it fo far furpaffed my moft fanguine expectations, both as to matter and manner, that I inftantly had it bound in a moft confpicuous manner, fo as that every one coming in could not fail to notice it; for it is far too good and unique to be facrificed to any individual monopoly. Even the author's name is unique and pre-Adamitifhly original, for I not only never heard it before, but never heard a name at all refembling it. But let it and its owner fpeak for themfelves; and to begin at the beginning, here is the title-page :—

" Young Gentleman and Lady's Privàte[1] Tutor. In Three Parts. The Firft Part contains a Preliminary Difcourfe on Moral and Social Duties, &c., viz. Piety, Wifdom, Prudence, Fortitude, Juftice, Temperance, Love, Friendfhip, Humanity, &c. The Second Part contains Rules for behaving Genteel [!] in all Stages of Life, of Behaviour to God, Parents, Company, Brothers, Sifters, Superiors, Equals, Inferiors, Teachers, Servants, in Company, at Meals, at Cards, &c. Walking

---

[1] No doubt the accent over the à in " privàte " is according to the author's ideas, to denote the *genteel* way of *publicly* pronouncing this egotiftical and unfociable word.

alone, With Company, &c. The Third Part contains Behaviour in the Dancing School, with Directions for Dancing a Minuet, Walking, Standing, Giving, Receiving, Bowing, and to make a Curtfey, &c. To which is added a Set of Figures of young Gentlemen and Ladies, adapted to the above Rules. Alfo Habits proper for Gentlemen and Ladies when Dancing, with Rules, and Cautions: and Figures fetting forth the true Ufe of the Fan. By Matthew TOWLE, Dancing Mafter, in Oxford. Printed for the Author,[1] MDCCLXX. Sold by J. Fletcher in Oxford; J. Fletcher in London; and by the Author's Father and Brother at all the Schools they attend."

> Then afk, "What's in a name?" indeed!
> Oh, fophiftry moft foul!
> Shakefpeare, could even *you* have lived
> If *your* name had been TOWLE?

Mr. Towle next proceeds to find great fault with the artift who furnifhed the plates for his valuable work; and not without reafon, I think, for as he juftly obferves, thefe faid plates are completely *difhed*, from a ftrange (but ftill perfectly original) defect in the anatomy of the figures and the perfpective of the inanimate

---

[1] This was, perhaps, a fupererogatory announcement, except as it additionally tends to prove that in no fingle particular has the uniform and fingular originality of this production been departed from.

objects reprefented; the former appearing for the moft part with the palms of their hands turned to the pofition that the backs generally occupy; and amid the vagaries of the latter are diftant garden walls and efpaliers infifting upon taking precedence of the mantlepieces and cabinets within the apartment, which, to a gentleman like Mr. Towle, devoting his energies to writing upon good manners, humility, and doing everything "*Genteel!*" muft have been particularly harrowing and diftreffing; fo that one cannot greatly wonder at the favage revenge he takes. But hear it in his own words, for

"None but himfelf can be his parallel."

One may almoft fancy that one fees him: his head thrown back, "quite genteel!" his eyes "in a fine frenzy rolling," his left hand on his hip, as with his right he prepared to make his fword leap from its fcabbard and fplit the unhappy *George Langly Smith*, of *Little Kirby Street, Hatton Garden, London*, as if he had been a Dunftable lark, predeftined to grilled bread crumbs and claret. But hufh! TOWLES LOQUITUR:

"The COPPER PLATES given in this Book coft *Seventeen Pounds, Six Shillings*, befides the expences of a *Law Suit*. . . . Engraved[1] by

---

[1] Query the lawfuit. The italics are Mr. Towles's, ftuck like larding-pins through and through the unhappy George Langly Smith.

George Langly Smith, in Little Kirby Street, Hatton Garden, London. The very great expence I have been at, I hope will atone and excuse me from censure for publishing these Copper Plates: and I doubt not, but my Subscribers will corroborate [!] *in their opinions with me* [!] that the following lines, taken from *Oldham*, are applicable to the above *Attempter* :—

> ' *To Mr. S. M——h.*
> ' Perhaps thou hop'dst that thy obscurity
> Should be thy safeguard, and secure thee free.
> No, wretch! *I* mean from thence to fetch thee out,
> Like sentenc'd felons to be dragg'd about ;
> Torn, mangled, and expos'd to scorn and shame,
> I mean to hang and gibbet up THY NAME!' "

After this, doubtless exhausted by the effort, exit TOWLE and enter subscribers :—

" WE, whose names are hereunto Subscribed, do approve the following Sheets, containing the first RUDIMENTS OF A POLITE EDUCATION, and recommend them, as very useful and proper to be introduced into all *Schools* and Families."

Here follows, not a single name, but a long blank sheet.

It is to be hoped, however, that the great TOWLE himself considered that by this strict preservation of the anonymous his subscribers were behaving " very genteel," and that the large white blank fpace left after their note of admiration was at once a delicate and a humorous way of intimating to him, that inftead of a vulgar, ordinary fubfcription, they gave him *carte blanche.*

Then comes the preface; but no, that is merely folemn ftupidity turned up with bad grammar, and therefore not worth tranfcribing; but there is a note appended to it, pointed out by a typographical hand, that really *is* noteworthy! Ecco!—

"The Author humbly hopes to find Favour, in the judgment of his fuperiors, in Age and Learning, and that they will view this Work as a *Juvenile Attempt,* and pafs over in filence all fuch Errors as may occur, unlefs of a Criminal Nature."!

True it is indeed, that not *only* the evil but fometimes "the good men do 'lives' after them;" for the foregoing would be an invaluable model note (with perhaps another fort of note inclofed in it) for every author to fend with his book to each of the *Reviews.* If it could not infure a puff, which depends more upon cliqueifm than even money or merit, ftill it could not fail to ward off a blow, except, perhaps, in the inftance of The "S——y R——w," which, even in the teeth of fo humble and touching an appeal, might be capable of this fort of growl :—

" In compliance with the author's requeſt, we paſs over his work in ſilence; but muſt proteſt againſt his having publiſhed it at all, as that appears to us fully to come under the denomination of what he terms 'Errors of a Criminal Nature.'"

As I have invited you, reader, to this *petit diner fin*, I ſhall now proceed to recommend to you ſome of the choice *morceaux* of the feaſt, not, however, helping you too largely; for *that* Mr. Towle, in his valuable rules " How to Behave *Genteel* at Meals," eſpecially deprecates in ſome ſarcaſtic (or, being at dinner, I ſhould ſay, cutting) remarks upon one Mr. *Lombum*, of whom he has informed poſterity that " though he eats but little, that is no reaſon he ſhould pick and cull the meat, and take juſt what he thinks proper. If any pudding comes to table you ſee he cuts it half, and eats not one fourth part of what he cuts.[1] So ſome of the company go without any, unleſs they will accept of his plate[!] If a fowl comes to table he takes the

---

[1] A very good plan of Mr. Lombum's for preventing the "company" coming again, and an evident proof that in claſſic Oxford in thoſe days they imitated the noble frugality of the ancients, when not ſacrificing at a great banquet, and might, like Seneca, have been ſurpriſed with a ſolitary meſs of lentil pottage, or, like Pliny the Younger, over a ſingle gentleman of a grey mullet and a cucumber.

prime pieces,[1] though he eats but little of them either. In fhort, he ferves everything fo that comes in his way. If a tart comes to table he cuts it, though nobody eats it,[2] and at the fame time he will put in the fpoon, take out the juice, and eat it with the fame fpoon, and after it has been in his mouth [!] he will put it into the tart again, for the perfons at table to help themfelves to, if they pleafe!"[3]

A grain of example being at all times better than a bufhel of precept, I fhall ftudioufly avoid giving you too large pieces of Mr. Towle's pudding (which I am furc you would *Lumbumife* if I did), and merely pick out the plums here and there. But before he expatiates on manner and deportment he has very properly two preliminary articles, entitled "OUR DUTY TO GOD AT HOME," and "OUR DUTY TO GOD OUT WALKING"!

In the firft of which he tells us (and *this* may not be altogether new to the readers of the

---

[1] Which really *is* foul, and *not* fair.

[2] If nobody eat it? Why, oh Magnus Towle! be fo fevere upon the taking ways of MR. LUMBUM? for by this it would appear that they *all* cut the tart.

[3] I knew it! There is always an adequate reafon for everything, however ftrange or unwonted, if people could only find it out, and this fpoony behaviour of MR. LUMBUM's fully accounts for the reft of "the company" exercifing their felf-denial with regard to the tart.

present generation), that it is our duty to God at home *to say our prayers!* but that " out of doors this is not necessary, as our duty there *is to behave genteel!* "[1]

* * * * *

But " Chapter XII. *Of Behaviour in Walking with Company*," though rather a long walk, is so very amusing, that it cannot possibly fatigue anybody.

" The next thing necessary," says Mr. Towle, " is to know how to behave in walking with company abroad.

" In the first place, consider who you are walking with and their RANK (with a big R !) and in how great a degree they are your superiors, or whether they are your equals. If they are your superiors in age, fortune, or birth, to them respect is due. By such considerations you

---

[1] It is quite clear from this that the terse TOWLE, evidently in advance of his age as he was, had no suspicion of open-air preaching then " looming in the future," or he would have ventilated the subject in his own inimitable manner; for in another part of his valuable work he tells us that our prayers in church are *not* acceptable to the Almighty "*unless we behave ourselves genteel*"! which he explains by warning the ladies against ogling through the sticks of their fans, and the men " doing *the like* over the rims of their hats," and " *both not omitting to bow or curtsey, polite and genteel, to their Superiors in the pew, every time they rise from kneeling at their devotions.*"

will always know how to addrefs and behave
politely to the Company you are with. It is impoffible that you fhould behave well or *genteel*,
and in a proper manner, unlefs you always take
a full view of them firft near[1] and attentive,
then you will be able to behave to every one according to their Rank. Should you fuffer yourfelf to neglect this rule, you will daily give
offence undefignedly, and by that means bring
yourfelf to Difgrace. It will alfo render you an
improper perfon for private Company as alfo
public. A man muft fhine in private Company,
even to appear in a decent manner in public.[2]

" I hope you will obferve what I have faid,
and then it will anfwer our purpofe. As I have
given you to underftand that it is neceffary for
you to know your Company,[3] I fhall fay no more
of it, but proceed. If you are walking with your
fuperiors, pay the refpect due to them, then will
you give fatisfaction.[4] It is your duty to give

---

[1] This really is making no allowance whatever for the
many perfons, as well as things, to whom
        " Diftance lends enchantment to the view."
[2] Towle! Towle! *nous avons changé tout cela.*
[3] Mr. Towle is here evidently labouring under a fort of
vulgar curiofity to know and find out who you are, employing
for that purpofe the ingredients of the proverbial receipt,
" Tell me your company and I'll tell you what you are."
[4] Here the author had evidently a retrofpective eye to
footmen.

them the wall in walking and to walk even with them, if there is not too great a number to walk abreaft [!] In this cafe you fhould agree to make two parties; then take care to let your elders walk firft; it is their place, therefore never attempt to take it of them, becaufe that would be behaving rude and ungenteel [!]; but when you are walking with your father or mother, governefs or teachers, then it is your place to go firft, and take care you walk upright and genteel.[!] In the next place you are to walk at a proper diftance, not too nigh nor too far off; the inconveniencies arifing from walking too nigh or too far off are difagreeable to them that walk firft, viz. if they are ladies you may in all probability tread upon their GOWNS, SAQUES, or TROLLOPEES [!], and very often may by an unguarded ftep tread upon their heels; this would not be very acceptable to the ladies. Should it be dark and dirty,[1] you would by going too nigh fplafh them all over; this they will think rude of you, although it might happen to any one in the dark. The only way to avoid thefe inconveniencies is

---

[1] In this counfel Mr. Towle (who appears to have been a perfon of fuch fubtle, fatirical wit as to make it almoft baffle detection,) muft have meant a fling at the Mohawks, who *were* addicted to walking in large parties abreaft in the dark and in the dirt, otherwife among no clafs were thefe miry tenebrious perambulations among the " Games and Paftimes of England."

not to walk too nigh them; about two yards is a proper diſtance; on the other hand you are not to exceed that ſpace, if you do you are guilty of bad manners to a great degree for walking ſix or ten yards behind your company, or as though you were talking of them or upon ſome ſubject that would be improper for them to hear, or as if you would rather walk by yourſelf. In the next place, it would be inconvenient to them to make you hear when they thought proper to ſpeak to you, which is very often the caſe, as you and every one muſt think. Be always attentive to what they ſay, and walk quietly and decently; avoid all coxcombical airs in walking, for this[1] *will give every one that ſees you an opportunity of knowing that you are a fool full as well as if they had been long acquainted with you.*[!] But I hope by this time you are ſo well acquainted with the rules of behaviour as to require my ſaying no more on ſelf-love and ſelf-conceit, ſo I will pro-

---

[1] Surely Towle the Terpſichorean does not, in his impenetrably diſguiſed irony, mean to ſay that by *not* giving himſelf coxcombical airs the mythological ſample young gentleman here invidiouſly pointed out would be anticipating the "courſe of time" by the revelation alluded to in the italiciſed paſſage that follows. No, no; it muſt only be one of thoſe grammatical errors into which he is conſtantly falling, in his laudable anxiety to avoid "criminal" ones, and he muſt have inadvertently ſubſtituted "this" for they, and ſo have achieved a *non*-ſenſe.

ceed in my difcourfe. Let all your converfation that paffes be fpoken in a foft tone of voice, in fuch a manner as your company may hear, but you are not obliged to fpeak fo loud that all the people in the ftreet may hear too; there is not any thing that points out low, ill bred perfons more than talking loud in the ftreet. [True, this, at all events.] If you fuffer yourfelf to converfe in that manner, fhould you be worth ten millions of money[!] you would be only one degree above any one in Billingfgate.[1] It is not money that makes the gentleman[2] always. Money does, I own, with fome bafe people; but what are they better than beafts of the field? No, not one jot; they even wrong their God of his due; then how can men expect to meet with civility and love from thofe who even make

---

[1] It might have been fo in *your* time, Towle, but other times other Towles, alias tactics, and *we* are wifer in our generation; for any one with even a tithe of that " *very genteel,*" becaufe by no means common, competency, TEN MILLIONS ! may not only talk as loud, but be as low as he pleafes. For this is really the Golden Age, or at leaft the age of gold. We read of ponies being fhod with golden fhoes in Auftralia, but there is nothing original in this; for a certain potentate of the Netherlands, ... fit to " mention to ears polite," has always had *his* hoofs fhod with gold when he wifhed to make fure of a good footing amongft us.

[2] Another error this in the Towlean philofophy, for the gentleman who makes money makes all other gentlemen bow down to him—or to his money, which is all the fame thing.

no fcruple to wrong their juft God for that falfe and bafe god, MONEY, and make a wrong ufe of it for it ever? Obferve thefe words :—
' It is eafier for a camel to go through the eye of a needle than for a rich man to enter into the kingdom of heaven.' Notwithftanding they have fuch a caution from the mouth of the Son of God, I may venture to fay [indeed, Towle, you may!] that there are fome people who make money their god, and none other do they worfhip. They are fworn enemies to humanity and to the poor, they even hate all kind of civility and politenefs, except what is fhewn to themfelves; that man is a fine gentleman who has money; they never inquire how he got it, or whom he wronged; what orphan or what widow; or whom he plundered or murdered; all wrongs are looked on as a perfection in him. The money makes the gentleman with fome perfons, but I hope it never will with you, for men who are fo inclined will even forfeit their own fouls, they will fell their daughters, in fhort, they will ftick at nothing to get money, and yet they can only have the ufe of it for this life." [1]

*　　*　　*　　*　　*

---

[1] Few perfons are fo *exigeant* as to require, or fo unreafonable as to expect, it longer. It is doubtful (mind, I do not venture to fay that it is *certain* he would not,) yes, it *is*

Mr. Towle then continues for four pages more in the same strain, but as it is also nearly *verbatim* the same as what I have just helped you to, allow me to recommend to you a few of his other *friandises.*

ARTICLE II.: or SECOND COURSE.

" When your company think proper to go into a house, church, or *any other place,*[1] you must let *them* go first; should it be *an* house where you are not acquainted then you are to stay till you are asked to walk in, which you

---

doubtful whether even the Marquis of ———— contemplates having his rental, his cheque-book, and the key of the cellar packed up in his coffin with him. But *quand même, cui bono?*

[1] Could Mr. Towle, by the stress he lays on "*any other place,*" have been alluding to the story of a certain testy old gentleman who upon one occasion, when about to take his diurnal drive, on being asked by the coachman, "Where to, sir?" responded in his gruffest tones, "To the D—l." The obedient Jehu made no reply, but gathered up his reins and proceeded. Several hours elapsed under the usual slow jog-trot family-coach pace, during which the old gentleman's choler decreased as his hunger increased, so, pulling the check, he cried out, "Where on earth are you going, John?" "Where you told me, sir," was the reply. John's master, being tickled at once by the fun and the phlegmatic philosophy of this answer, said, with a latent twinkle in his eye and an expression of bland remonstrance on his lip, "Well, but how will you manage about yourself when you get there?" "Oh, no need to trouble about *me,* sir. *I shall back you in.*"

may depend upon it they *will do*. [Query, " You will be."] When you *are* afked to walk in, take off your hat in your left hand, bow, and go in; if they afk you to fit down, do it, and at the fame time bow or curtfey, faying, ' Thank you, fir,' or ' madam.' Take your feat at THE BOTTOM OF THE ROOM, if you have not a place told you to fit in; fhould the room not be full of company then you are to take the bottomeft feat next your company; but you will have a chair placed for you to fit in, or at leaft there ought to be one. You muft be cautious here in your behaviour, never to fpeak unlefs you are fpoken to, then addrefs them Sir or Madam, as I have given you inftructions before how to addrefs every one, according to their quality and fortune.

" Always be concife in your opinion, exprefs your fentiments in few words, and as diftinct as poffible. [Very good advice.] When your company think proper to go let your fuperiors go out firft; then take leave of the company that are in the room in a genteel manner, paying a juft refpect to them all. When you come to the ftreet door bow to the gentleman or lady that waits on you to the door; *for you may depend on't they are very genteel people who wait on their guefts to the door*. I would not have you mifunderftand me wrong, and think that I mean they are rich, and the like.[1] No; I mean that they know how to behave polite and genteel. If they come to the door, bow with all the refpect you are mafter of, faying, 'Madam,' or 'Sir, I am very forry to give you this trouble.' And again, fhould there be no fervant to open the door, if you are well acquainted with the houfe, fooner than give the mafter or miftrefs the trouble to open the door, fay, in a polite manner, 'Madam,' or 'Sir, give me leave to open the door, we can do very well without giving you the trouble to attend us to the door;' but if they infift on it do not difpute with them, but take care not to detain them at the door, leaft they catch cold thereby.

" Now you are in the ftreets again, if you fee anything that may appear furprifing do not ftop to look at it, but look at it as you go on; fhould you ftop, as I have faid before, it would be rude, but I fhall forbear to fay more, as I have faid enough before.[2] You are never to call after any of your acquaintance in the public ftreet, but if you fee any one that you want to fpeak to go up

---

[1] Every one knows there is *nothing* like being rich, therefore what *can* " rich and the *like*" poffibly mean? Perhaps fome of our modern writers who affect thofe moft deteftable of all vulgarifms of the 15th, 16th, 17th, and 18th centuries, " the like," and " fuch like," may be able to tell, but I really cannot.

[2] I think fo too.

to him firft.[1] It is not genteel, neither is it polite, to point[2] at any one, or to point in at any fhop window. Should you fee any thing pleafing to the company and would communicate it, fpeak decently thus : 'Gentlemen,' or 'Ladies, if you pleafe to look this way here is fomething that will pleafe you ;' but forbear to fay 'Look yonder,' or 'Look there,' for if you *was* to exprefs yourfelf fo it would be imitating oyfter girls or boys ; for none but thofe fort of people ufe fuch kind of language. In the next place, you are to avoid dreffing yourfelf in the ftreet.[3] Poffibly you may afk what I mean by *that ?* But to fave you the trouble of afking I will do my endeavours to inform you. In the firft place, I mean that I would have you appear decent as you walk along, free from affectation, pride, *and the like.* But in order that you may underftand me better I will give you an example, by fhewing you that infufferable Fop, Mr. GAUDY. This is a fop, of whom I will do my endeavours to draw the outlines, as near as poffible, but it would be a work

---

[1] This is generally confidered to be a neceffary preliminary.

[2] Of courfe, this does not apply to pointers with regard to partridges ; therefore it is to be hoped, even if not "genteel," they will be too well bred to confider this remark perfonal.

[3] A bedroom cannot be too airy, but certainly fuch an *al frefco* dreffing-room as the ftreet would be anything but defirable, to fay nothing of the impropriety of fuch a proceed-

of time to draw a juft PIECE of him,[1] but I think you will have an opportunity of feeing him if you will walk this way. O, now you fee him, there he is! now you will fee fifty different motions betwixt here and the bottom of the ftreet; now you fee him beholding himfelf! now he looks behind him, to fee who is looking at him; every one that looks at him he thinks admires him;[2] if a lady looks at him he imagines fhe admires him as fomething more than flefh and blood and real nature. There! obferve him rubbing his hands, beholding them with admiration. Now you fee he fmiles with the pleafing thoughts that his hands begin to make him amends for all the trouble and expenfe he has been at *about his hands!* Ah, what makes you look at me fo? what do you wonder at? you will fay, For heaven's fake, what expenfe can he have been at about his hands?

---

ing. But this, perhaps, is what is meant in the old plays of the Congreve and Wycherly fchool, by having "the *airs* of a man, or woman, of *quality*." *Now* the only airs of a ftreet are thofe ground on a barrel organ.

[1] Now really, unartiftic ignoramufes might have fuppofed that it was eafier to draw a *piece* of Mr. GAUDY than even the outline, though, as a whole, he might have required all the vermilion and gamboge lavifhed on his funfets and funrifes by the late Mr. Turner, R.A.

[2] This diftemper, oh Towle! I can affure you, is quite as much an epidemic among "gents" in pegtops in our day as it was among Gaudys in periwigs in yours.

Why, I will tell you, thefe kind of people lie in lamb-fkin gloves,[1] and go to a great expenfe in buying waters to wafh their hands in to make them look fair. But obferve him pulling down his fhirt-fleeves;[2] now placing his ruffles, there, now his neckcloth, now his hat. But obferve that porter who comes along; it is ten to one that he hits that thing on his fhoulder againft him, for you fee he looks likely enough to do it, for he pays no refpect to perfons. Ah! ah! now you fee, juft I faid, fo it is; you fee he has *dif-obliged*[!] Mr. Gaudy's hair, which was fo curioufly dreffed, and fplafhed the dirt all over him too. That is very monftrous indeed, and you fee the rogue fmiles, as if he had done it for the joke's fake. Poor fop, quite out of patience, you fee; he takes his handkerchief to wipe his ftockings, and by hanging down his hands makes them red; what a pity indeed to have his hands fo much changed, *all along with fuch a fellow!* Notwith-ftanding this misfortune, you fee he is eaten up with affectation; now his fhirt is not right, now he is placing his neckcloth, now his finger is in his hair, now he looks behind him, now his coat-fleeves are pulled down, they are not low enough,

---

[1] Verily, this is only a venial offence, feeing that fome perfons will lie in anything and through everything.

[2] Surely, oh Towle the Terrible! you would not have him pull them up?

and if you were to follow him all day he would never be rightly dressed. Observe the first operator's shop for the hair, if he does not go in there; there, now he goes into the shop. Poor creature ! you see he is quite sick, his face shows he is ready to faint with vexation.   Now we will leave him there, to undergo a fatigue for an hour and a half."

Grateful in the extreme to Mr. Gaudy for having gone into the hairdresser's shop (though I don't exactly see how *that* was to get the mud off his stockings), I will now proceed, dear reader, to place before you the last of this feast of fragments, in the form of a panegyric and a philippic, by the masterly hand of Towle.   The former you may consider as a *soufflé*, winding up our repast, and the latter as ginger ice, it is at once so cool and yet so spicy.

"Master Loutes.

"a panegyric.

" Compliance is an honourable disposition of the mind [!] where it is truly united in *an* humane heart. Happy is that man who hath it in his possession; he is sure to be respected and esteemed in company ; he condescends to oblige others in never contradicting their desires, if honourable and consistent with reason.

" This sort of complaisance makes him agreeable.[1] He is loved, becaufe he is of an eafy, flexible temper : his will feems not his own. Every defire of his friends would he do, and all that was in his power, in order that they might be happy. MASTER LOUTES is of this complaifant turn. You cannot look at what you want[2] before he is up and fetches it, before you have time to afk. He doth it with fo much good nature and eafe, that you would imagine he was upon fome peculiar bufinefs of his own, and all the time he is entirely ftudying what may pleafe you. So fweet is the difpofition of MASTER LOUTES, there is not one day paffes but he diftinguifhes himfelf by his complaifance and fweet temper."

> Once on a time lived Anacharfis Cloots,[3]
> Who about the human race did howl;
> But more than bleft, thrice happy, Mafter Loutes,
> You—you have found an orator in TOWLE!

---

[1] There cannot be a doubt of it.

[2] Then Mr. Loutes *père* muft have been greatly to be pitied, as it is evident from this that Mafter Loutes was *up to everything*.

[3] Pronounced Clouts.

An Invidious Philippic,
not against Mother Church, but against Mothers at Church.

" 'My little ladies, I will here give you friendly advice. I hope you will not take it amiss, as I think it my duty so to do in everything that lies in my power.

" ' 'When you are seated in your place at Church do not get up again till the service is begun; then rise, place your eyes on your prayer-book, and there keep them till such time as that part of the service is over. If you, on the contrary, get up and look about you, or through your fan at any one, you will be guilty of a breach of that modesty which is peculiar to your sex, or ought to be.'

" S. ' Yes, sir, I do not dispute your judgment, but I have seen my mamma and Lady *Mears* do so.'

" M. ' Something extraordinary might happen. Very possibly your mamma could not see for the sun, that might be the cause of it; and Lady *Mears* is always laughing, she being sensible of the crime, though she has not prudence enough to avoid it; therefore she is ashamed to show her face.'

" S. ' Yes, sir, my mamma hath done it, that

ſhe might look at L——y G——d's ſilk gown. She hath bid me do ſo too. She bought me and herſelf a fan each, with holes in the mounts on purpoſe. She can tell all or moſt of all the ladies' dreſſes that are in church. There is not a ſtranger but what ſhe knows who they are with, and what they had on, and who ſuch and ſuch gentlemen looked at.'

" M. 'But my little lady, you may be miſtaken. This notice ſhe may take when the ſervice is over.'

" S. 'No, ſir, my mamma bid me obſerve laſt Sunday, in the middle of the ſermon, the parſon's diamond ring and his white hand.'

" M. 'Miſs, I will allow that you might underſtand your mamma as ſuch, but I'm inclined to think that you are under a miſtake. She might tell you to mind the parſon and not play with your hand and ring, for I am of an opinion your mamma is of a more ſedate turn, or ought to be, after being the mother of ten children,[1] ſo

---

[1] In claſſing the prolific among the ſedatives, does Mr. Towle mean to imply that ten children are a ſort of maternal henbane? But mark the mingled prudence and fine irony of this paſſage: " I am of *an* opinion that your mamma is of a more ſedate turn, *or ought to be!*" Then the ſubtle, Bellerephon plan he adopts for letting the mothers know what their tell-tale daughters ſay of them, by the way in which he begs the queſtion in theſe dialogues.

I hope you are under a miftake; but my dear child, do not think I doubt your veracity, only you might miftake the thing.' "

There are about twenty pages more, all in the fame ftrain—a fine and perfectly parliamentary one: in which he denounces all the impious horrors of the mamma's ogling propenfities in church, and then fuddenly pulls up to tell " the little lady" that not for a moment does *he* fuppofe *her* mamma capable of anything of the kind.

But the moft charming part of this truly charming work is Mr. Towle's modefty, in what he himfelf would call " taking the bottomeft place" [!] in the different eulogiums fcattered throughout it; for it will be remembered that he was a dancing-mafter, and although, after fetting forth all the gliding graces of the minuet, he expatiates eloquently on thofe lefs dignified but more infpiriting French dances, the *Rigadoon*, the *Louvre*, the *Courant*, and the *Borée*, and animadverts upon ladies' dreffes, not fparing their *facques*, *night-gowns*,[1] and *trollopees*, telling them

---

[1] At that time, what we call evening dreffes were always called *night-gowns*, as they were in Elizabeth's time, when men's dreffing-gowns were alfo called *night-gowns;* hence the following entry by her Majefty's " privy purfe:" " To a fine Murray *Velut*, frizzed on the wrong fide, chofe by her Highnefs as a night-gown for my Lord of Leicefter."

how they are attired, or at leaft *how they ought to be !* (that favourite claufe of his), and finds ruffles "marvellous proper" things for grown-up ladies, but abominations for "little miffes,"— thereby, I fuppofe, meaning to fay, that young ladies fhould never be ruffled. Still, he never fays one word in praife of the charming art of which he is a profeffor till the very climax of his exhortations, when to be fure, to make up for loft time, he *does* "come it rather ftrong" by breaking out into the following exclamation, for which he has not even the kindnefs to prepare his readers, as we were once prepared for and warned againft the French invafion :—

"I believe it is beyond a doubt that dancing is acceptable to God; and as a *proof* obferve thefe words—'*Praife Him in the cymbals and dances.*'"

And not another word does he add to this ftartling announcement. How could he, without making an anti-climax?

But foon after, both in rhyme and reafon, he gives fome very good advice to the fairer part of the creation, as to their choice of colours;

> One would think it was Minerva's owl
> Blandly preaching through the lips of Towle.

"There are different colours," faith he, as fome gentlemen among the Latin poets have faid before him, "that agree with different complexions, and this is a matter really worth the ladies' obſervation; but this ſubject I will leave to the ladies' own inſpection," [query, ſelection?] "only giving them the opinion of a poet that now lies before me."

Of *courſe*, as it is an underſtood thing that poets excel in fiction, the poet *lies* before him.

> "Let the fair nymph in whoſe plump cheeks are ſeen
> A conſtant bluſh, be clad in verdant green;[1]
> In ſuch a dreſs the ſportive ſea-nymphs go,
> So in their graſſy beds freſh roſes blow.
>
> "The laſs whoſe ſkin is like the hazel brown,
> With brighter yellow ſhould o'ercome her own;
> But the fair maid in whoſe pale cheeks of ſnow
> No bluſhes riſe nor blooming roſes glow
>
> "Far above all ſhould potent ſcarlet fly,
> And ſooner chuſe the ſable's mournful dye:[2]
> So the pale moon ſtill ſhines with pureſt light,
> Cloath'd in the duſky mantle of the night."

One more *bonne-bouche*, and then Magnus Towle may be removed.

"The dreſs is the next thing to be conſidered.

---

[1] "Blue or yellow, or light green, *blue yellow* (again) ſtraw, or ſtriped ſilks of the ſame colours."—TOWLE.

[2] "Or Pompadour." Strange advice, Mr. Towle, as Pompadour is orange; certainly *not* a becoming tint to perſons of a pale complexion.

Every young lady ought to be dreffed genteel; that is, in filk or linen, with linen according to it; [?] the ftockings filk or cotton, the fhoes filk, or morocco, or ftuff, neatly made; for the feet are more the object of notice in *dancing* than any other part in *dancing*.

" Each young lady ought to be dreffed according to her age. Whatever ladies wear ought to fit them,[1] for not anything is a greater difadvantage than clothes badly fitted. Some mammas take a pleafure in feeing the fhoulders of their children left bare, even down to the elbows, but I promife them that there are many ill confequences attending it; but perhaps they will fay it is loofe and genteel. Loofe, indeed, it is, and indecently genteel too. On the other hand, they may plead for an excufe that they do not love to fee their children confined about the fhoulders, and that it gives them room to grow. *That* is my opinion too, even till their fhoulders touch their ears, and *learns* them to grow fluttifh and ungenteel. I would recommend to thofe who would have their children appear decent and genteel, to take care that their children's flips fit very exactly on the fhoulders, for it is of infinite fervice to thofe who are inclinable to

---

[1] Though this is true, yet it does not apply to truth, fince *ex nihilo nihil* fit.

grow high-ſhouldered—it helps to keep their ſhoulders down in their proper place. I ſhall further recommend gathered tuckers as a decent and abſolutely neceſſary part of dreſs; it alſo adds to a genteel fall[1] from the ſhoulders. Some ladies may ſay : 'Oh ſir! my daughter muſt appear agreeable, ſo fine a ſkin as ſhe's got.' Ladies, I agree with you; a fine ſkin is agreeable, but decency is much more ſo, eſpecially if it add beauty to the wearer.

"Hats, tippets, and ſhades [?] are not to be worn in dancing; *it is* [!] impertinent, awkward, and clowniſh. The dreſs of the neck I leave every one to dreſs as they think proper (only thoſe who have long necks I adviſe them to wear ſomething, as that is genteel.)

"The next thing that demands our attention is, the dreſs of the head. For young ladies from three to fourteen years old, a feather, a flower, egret, or *ribbond*, or pompoon; theſe are proper for dancing in. Ladies above this age may do as they pleaſe,[2] only I think the

---

[1] Query: Would Mr. Towle have conſidered the Falls of Niagara as genteel, or too much of a fall, ſo as to come under the category of the foregone philippic?

[2] I rather think that *that* age, viz., when ladies may do as they pleaſe, has not yet arrived, or even ſet out; for though "a good time" has long been announced as "coming" for

prefent fafhion is very becoming,—I mean the rolls, &c."[1]

Now we will go upftairs to coffee; and I hope, reader, you will think that "Le véritable Amphitryon eft celui chez qui l'on—danfe!"

---

the "boys," there has not been a word faid about any fuch "welcome gueft" being *en route* for the girls.

[1] Mr. Towle does not fpecify *what* rolls, but of courfe he means *French rolls.*

ON THE COMPARATIVENESS OF GREATNESS.

WE read in the old Chronicles, that " In the firſt of Queen Mary, the braveſt ſhip in England, called 'The Great Harry' (by reaſon of its having been built in Henry VIII.'s time, and called after him), was burnt through negligence at Woolwich. It was 1,000 tons; and the people did think that the ſudden deſtruction which had overtaken it [!] was a judgment of God's diſpleaſure at man's preſumption to build ſo mighty a veſſel, to try and maſter as it were His winds and waves, which can only be maſtered by Himſelf."

The logic of this is rather Hibernian; for once granted that we may, do, and have launched hazel-nut and walnut ſhells on God's great ocean, there can ſurely be no additional ſin in increaſing the ſize of theſe nut-ſhell crafts to that of cocoa-nuts, or even of calabaſhes. We ſmile at theſe little homœopathic and opaque ſuperſtitions of our forefathers, and yet in this our boaſted nineteenth century, when we have achieved a more rare wonder than Mr. Rarey, by taming the lightning to drive in our MAIL PHAETONS, and when, if we have not actually " put a girdle round the earth in forty minutes," we *have* thrown a chain acroſs the Atlantic, ſtill, we have *not* outgrown, we have only changed the *venue* of our ſuperſtition; for when the " Great Eaſtern " exceeded the " Great Harry " by 22,600 tons,[1] it was not its coloſſal ſize that alarmed the pious ſuſceptibilities of the " Britiſh

---

[1] The burden of the " Great Eaſtern " is 23,600 tons! But the mighty " Great Eaſtern " itſelf pales (in all but ſize) before the *liburnæ* of Caligula, of which Suetonius gives ſuch a glowing deſcription; thoſe fairy-tale like barks, made of the perfumed cedar, with their party-coloured ſilken ſails, ſilver cordage, purple and gilded ivory prows, their porticoes, ſaloons, and baths, their fragrant and blooming gardens, luxuriant vines and variety of fruit-trees, in which triumphs of art over nature the luxurious monſter, the to " laſcivious tunings " of golden lutes, would loll the ſultry hours away, as he ſkirted the ceſtus ſhores of lovely Campania. Theſe *liburnæ*, moreover, appear to have been a ſort of ſteamboats with the ſteam left out, for they were impelled by three wheels on each ſide, but without touching the water, conſiſting of eight ſpokes jutting out from the wheel about a hand's breadth, and ſix oxen within, which, by turning an engine, worked the wheels, the revolutions of which, driving the

Public," as a preſumptuous braving of Omnipotence, but ſimply its original name of the "*Leviathan*"!!! which, why or wherefore folly only knows (for it would indeed be a metaphyſical puzzle to try and trace the origin of ſuch an aſſociation of ideas), but certain it is, that in the eſtimation of theſe worthies the name being ſelected from the Bible, with a ſtrange inverſe holineſs (?) on that account they ſeemed to conſider profane, though no doubt, had it been chriſtened the "Crocodile" they would not have winced a letter; and yet Fry conſiders that the whole deſcriptions of the "behemoth," "leviathan," and "crocodile," in Job, all tally ſo remarkably in every particular and peculiarity, as to be ſuppoſed to mean one and the ſame monſter; and "behemoth," at ch. xl. ver. 19, is ſpoken of as "unequalled," and "leviathan" at ch. xli. ver. 33, is alſo ſpoken of as unequalled, which cannot be ſaid of either of two different animals or of two diſtinct magnitudes; and moreover, the deſcription of the habits of the crocodile, given by all naturaliſts and travellers, exactly agrees with thoſe imputed to the "leviathan" or "behemoth" by Job. But as I ſaid before, ALL

water backward, impelled theſe *liburnæ* forward with ſuch force and ſpeed that no three-oared galley was able either to keep up with or to reſiſt them.

greatneſs, whether moral, phyſical, intellectual, or ſocial, that of fame or that of conventionality or chance, is wholly and ſolely Comparative, not to ſay geographical, and the POSITIVE has, it is to be feared, very little to do with its appreciation among them. Further, I contend that time and place are great make-weights, and that the local has much to do with the laudatory. "GREAT" was "Diana of the Epheſians," on *earth;* ſhe ſhone rather leſs as Luna in the celeſtial regions; dwindled into an "unprotected female" as Proſerpine, in the infernal ones; became poſitively obnoxious as Hecate; and if, under the travelling title of Trivia, ſhe had occaſionally at ſome ſlippery croſs-road a dog, a lamb, or a little honey offered to her in the way of propitiation by a few timorous wayfarers, ſtill, that was but poor compenſation for her former ſplendour. However, ſhe always had the advantage of her former divinity hanging about her; unlike mere mortals under a reverſe of fortune, for they, poor wretches, invariably go to the dogs, inſtead of getting even a ſingle dog brought to them. Then as a check to all earthly greatneſs (or as Mr. Towle would ſay, what at leaſt *ought to ſuch*), comes DEATH! with his grim gambols, playing at bowls with crowns, ſceptres, wiſe heads and wicked ones, and after his paſtime, banqueting alike on golden hearts that never beat but to good and glorious motives, or on grovelling, narrow ones, that never glowed with even ONE generous impulſe.

Edward III., "the glorious conqueror," as he was called in his own day, and certainly one of the moſt popular of Engliſh kings, "fell," as the chroniclers tell us, "into his laſt ſickneſs at Richmond. When he was drawing on, his concubine, Alice Pierce, came, and took the rings from his fingers, leaving him gaſping for breath. And the officers of his court rifled him of whatſoever they could. A prieſt, lamenting the king's miſery, that among all his ſervants had none to aſſiſt him in his laſt moments, exhorted him to repent and implore the mercy of God. The king had loſt his ſpeech, but at theſe words uttered his mind imperfectly, and made ſigns of contrition; but his voice failing him in pronouncing the name of Jeſus, he yielded up the ghoſt."

A little goodneſs, however humble, unknown, and inſignificant, at this laſt ſupreme hour, that *muſt* ſtrike for *all*, is worth a world-wide greatneſs, falſely ſo called. Had Edward III. been a better man, though a leſs great king, that is, had he eſchewed flatterers and avoided Alice Pierces "*and the like*," he might have died with his rings on his fingers and his pockets unſcathed by the rifle corps movement. And he ſhould have done ſo; for the ſpark of ſacred fire was there, had he but kindled inſtead of ſmothering it. Alas, poor human nature! what know we of MOST of all—the droſs through which our ſpirit works its way, upward and onward, to its HOME? As in the chemiſtry of common things, the moſt heterogeneous rubbiſh goes to fine wine, jelly, or coffee, and bring them ultimately to that tranſlucent purity that conſtitutes their perfection, may it not be the ſame with ourſelves? or as Wordsworth finely expreſſes it in thoſe magnificent lines of his—

> " Duſt as we are, the immortal ſpirit grows
> Like harmony in muſic: there is a dark
> Inſcrutable workmanſhip that reconciles
> Diſcordant elements, makes them cling together
> In one ſociety. How ſtrange, that all
> The terrors, pains, and early miſeries,
> Regrets, vexations, laſſitudes, interfuſed
> Within my mind, ſhould e'er have borne a part,
> And that a needful part, in making up
> The calm exiſtence that is mine, when I
> Am worthy of myſelf! Praiſe to the end."[1]

Among the *vulgar errors* Sir Thomas Browne has omitted to note, is that *very* vulgar one of ſuppoſing AMBITION to be a noble paſſion; when, on the contrary, it is one of *the* moſt

---

[1] " The Prelude and Growth of a Poet's Mind," an Autobiographical Poem, by William Wordsworth. Moxon.

vulgar of paſſions, from being the moſt ſelfiſh, mean, ſordid, unſcrupulous, and conſequently un-chivalrous, of all the paſſions; for truly, moſt ambitious men may be accurately ſummed up in Lowell's lines—

> " He had been noble, but ſome great deceit
> Had turn'd his better inſtinct to a vice;
> He ſtrove to think the world was all a cheat,
> That power and fame were cheap at any price;
> That the ſure way of being ſhortly great
> Was ever to play life's game with loaded dice:
> Since he had tried the honeſt plan, and found
> That vice and virtue differ'd but in ſound."

And all this terrible ſelf-ſacrifice of body and ſoul—for ſuch it *literally* is—to find *all* VANITAS VANITATUM, OMNIA VANITAS!

UPON THE GREAT DIFFERENCE OF THE SAME CIRCUMSTANCES IN OUR OWN CASE AND THAT OF OTHERS,

WHICH ALWAYS HAS EXISTED, AND IT IS TO BE FEARED ALWAYS WILL EXIST.

Written juſt after the Diſaſter of Sedan.

" Meus mihi, ſuus cuique eſt carus."—Plautus.

OW ſtrange and unforeſeen are the revenges which " the whirligig of Time" brings about ! and in moſt of them how inciſively Nemeſis points the moral ! At the preſent criſis it is curiouſly intereſting, to read by the glare of the torch of diſcord of the preſent Franco-Germanic war, Voiture's letter of panegyric on Cardinal Richelieu a brace of centuries ago, upon *his* annexation of Alſace and Lorraine; *the* letter in fact which Monſieur Perrault compared to Pliny's panegyric upon Trajan. Well, compariſons are proverbially

odious, and sometimes even odorous, as Mrs. Mal-
aprop has it; but if the shade of Pliny retains a
shadow of the good sense he possessed in the
flesh it will only smile and glide on, remembering
that the comparison was made by a Frenchman.
But the letter itself contains such good advice to
victors as well as vanquished, that it is a thousand
pities that all Germany, as well as all France,
cannot spare time from the glorious work of
butchering each other, to " read, mark, learn, and
inwardly digest" it. *Cela pose*, I will give a trans-
lation of the letter *in extenso* :—

" I am not one of those, as you would seem to
imply, who delight to improve all my Lord Cardinal's actions into miracles and waft his praises
beyond due bounds, and who, while they would
make the world believe well of him, sacrifice all regard to credibility. On the other hand, I am not
of such a base detracting nature as to hate a man
merely because he is above the rest of the world,
neither will I suffer myself to be carried away by
popular prepossessions, which I know generally
speaking to be unjust. I consider him with an
unprejudiced judgment, where passion has nothing
to do on the one side or the other; and I behold
him with the same eyes that posterity will behold
him. And certainly *two hundred years hence*,[1] when

---

[1] M. Voiture did *not* foresee that Lorraine and Alsace

thofe who look upon him after us fhall read in our hiftory that the great Cardinal de Richelieu demolifhed Rochelle, confounded the heretics, and by one fingle *coup de main* took thirty or forty of their cities all at once—when they fhall come to know, that at the time of his adminiftration the Englifh were beaten and repulfed, Picardy conquered, Caffel relieved, Lorraine annexed to France, the greateft part of Alfatia fubjugated by us, the Spaniards defeated at Vellaine and Avien; I fay, that when they fhall find that *while he* prefided over our affairs France had not one neighbour over whom fhe did not gain fome important victory or town, if they have the leaft drop of French blood in their veins and any love for the honour of their country, can they read thefe things without having a great love for him? And do you think they will love or efteem him the lefs becaufe the payments of the Hôtel de Ville came in fomewhat of the floweft? or becaufe fome new offices were erected? Great things cannot be done without great expenfe, and to cramp them for want of money is to maim their execution. But if we are to look upon a kingdom as immortal, and to confider the advantages it will reap in future ages, as if they were *actually prefent*, let us compute how

---

would be wrefted back from the great Cardinal's dead grafp by a German Richelieu.

many millions this man, who they pretend has ruined France, has saved her by the bare taking of Rochelle? which town two thousand years hence, in all the minorities of our kings, upon every discontent of our nobles, and upon all occasions of revolt, would most certainly have rebelled, and have entailed upon us a perpetual expense. Our kingdom had only two enemies to fear: the Huguenots and the Spaniards. My Lord Cardinal no sooner entered upon affairs but he immediately resolved to ruin both? Was it possible for him to form more glorious or more advantageous designs? He has happily effected the one, but not completed the other. However, if he has failed in his first design, those who now cry out that it was a rash unreasonable resolution to pretend to attack and humble the power of Spain, and that experience had sufficiently shown it, yet would they not have been as forward to condemn his design of ruining the Huguenots? Would they not have told us that we ought not to have embarked in an enterprise wherein three of our kings [Francis II., Charles IX., and Henry III.] had miscarried, and which the late king [Henri Quatre] did not so much as think of? And would they not have concluded, as erroneously as they do in this other affair, that the thing was not feasible merely because it was not already done? But let us consider, I beseech you, if it was his or Fortune's fault, that he has not as yet accomplished the design. Let us see what method he took to effect it, and what engines he set in motion. Let us examine whether he has failed much in felling that mighty tree, the House of Austria, and has not shaken the very root of the trunk, whose two branches covered the north and the west, and overshadowed the rest of the earth. He went as far as the northern pole to find out that hero[1] who seemed predestined to lay the axe to it and bring it to the ground. It was his skill, combined with his thunder, which filled all Germany with fire and desolation, and the noise of which echoed through the world. But when this tempest was dispersed and Fate had turned away the impending blow, did *he* stop short in his course or cease his designs? and did he not bring the Empire lower than it had been brought by the losses of the battle of Leipsic and that of Lützen? His astuteness and energy raised us up suddenly an army of forty thousand men in the heart of Germany, with a general at the head of them who was master of all the great qualities requisite to bring about a revolution in any state. If the King of Sweden threw himself into danger more than became a person of his design and rank, and if the Duke of Friedland, by over-delaying his enterprise, suffered it to get wind and be discovered, was it possible for the

---

[1] Gustavus Adolphus.

Cardinal either to charm the bullet which killed the former in the midſt of victory, or render the latter impervious to the blows of a *partiſan ?* And if after this diſmal blow, to complete the ruin of our affairs, the generals who commanded the armies of our allies before Nördlingen gave battle at an unſeaſonable time, was it poſſible for the Cardinal, who was above two thouſand leagues from the ſpot, to change this reſolution, and check the unadviſable raſhneſs of thoſe who, for an empire that would have been the certain price of victory, would not ſtay three days longer? Thus you ſee it was impoſſible to ſave the Houſe of Auſtria and hinder the execution of the Cardinal's deſigns, which ſome perſons pretend were ſo raſh that had not Fortune wrought three ſurpriſing miracles, that is to ſay, three great events, which in all probability it would have been thought never could have happened—I mean the death of the King of Sweden, that of the Duke of Friedland, and the loſs of the battle of Nördlingen—you will tell me he has no reaſon to complain of Fortune for croſſing him in this, ſince ſhe had ſerved him ſo faithfully in all his other deſigns; ſince ſhe put places into his hands without his ſo much as laying ſiege to them ; and ſince alſo by her favour he commanded armies ſo ſucceſsfully without the leaſt experience to direct him, ſhe leading him always as it were by the hand, and bringing him ſafe out of the greatest perils into which he had thrown himself, and made him appear, bold, wise, and prescient without any merit of his. Let us therefore behold him in his evil fortune, and examine if even then he evinced less boldness, wisdom, and foresight. Our affairs were in no very good posture in Italy, and as it is the destiny of France to win battles and lose armies, ours was exceedingly diminished ever since the last victory we had gained over the Spaniards. We had not much better luck before Dôle, where the length of the siege made us apprehend its ill success, when we received news that the enemy had entered Picardy, that they had at the first onset taken Cassel, Castelet, and Corbie; and that these three places, which ought to have held out eight months, scarcely held out as many days. All was in fire and ashes to the banks of the Oise; we might behold from our suburbs the smoke of the villages which the enemy had burnt. All the world was alarmed at this sudden progress, and the capital city of our kingdom was in the highest consternation. In the midst of these calamities advices came from Burgundy that the siege of Dôle was raised, and from Xaintoigne that fifty thousand peasants were up in arms, and that it was feared the infection would spread to Poitou and Guienne. Ill news came pouring upon us from all parts, the whole face of heaven was overcast, the tempest invaded us from

every fide, and we had not the leaft profpect of
good fortune to fupport us in thefe extremities.
We could not perceive daylight through the
fmalleft aperture. But in all this darknefs did the
Cardinal fee lefs clearly than at other times? Did he
lofe either his judgment or refolution? And during
this ftorm, did he not always keep the rudder in
one hand and the compafs in the other? Did he call
out for the long-boat to fave himfelf? And if the
great veffel which he fteered was deftined to be
caft away, did he not fhow that he was the firft
man who refolved to perifh? Was it Fortune
that delivered him out of this labyrinth, or his
own prudence and magnanimity? Our enemies
were within fifteen leagues of Paris, and his were
in the town; he received daily advices that cabals
were held and defigns formed to ruin him; France
and Spain were, if I may fo exprefs myfelf, joined
in a confpiracy againft him alone. Now amidft
all thefe threatening circumftances and concur-
rences, in the midft of fo dreadful and black a
conjunction, how did this man look, whom they
pretended would be caft down upon the leaft ill
fuccefs, and who, as they gave out, had fortified
Havre de Grace on purpofe to make it a place of
retreat in cafe of any difafter? He does not go
one ftep backwards for all this. He is taken
up with the dangers of the ftate, and not with
his own; and all the alteration we could obferve

in him at this time was, that whereas he never used to go abroad without two hundred guards, he now walked out every day attended only by five or six gentlemen. All the world must own that an adverfity fupported with fo good a grace and with fo much courage is to be preferred to victory and profperity itfelf. He did not appear to me fo great and victorious, even when he made his entry into Rochelle, as then; and the daily vifits he made to the arfenal were, in my opinion, more glorious to him than his famous expedition on the other fide of the mountains, when he took Pignerol and Sufa. Therefore, let me conjure you to open your eyes and to prepare for beholding fo bright an object. Lay afide your averfion to the man who is fo happy in revenging himfelf upon his enemies, and ceafe to wifh ill to him who knows how to turn it to his glory by bearing himfelf fo undauntedly under it. Leave your party before they leave you, as a great number of the great Cardinal's enemies have done, who were converted by the laft miracle they faw him perform. If the war fhould ceafe, as there is reafon to hope it will, he'll foon find a way to gain the reft over to his fide. Being fo wife as he is, he muft certainly know, after fo much experience, what is beft for us, and will aim all his defigns fo as to make us the moft flourifhing people in the world, after he has made us the moft formidable.

" He will content himfelf with an ambition that is to be preferred before all others, and which is practifed but by few: I mean, to make himfelf the beft and moft beloved man in the kingdom, and not the greateft and moft feared. He knows that the nobleft and the moft lafting conquefts are thofe of the heart and the affections; that laurels are barren plants, which yield nothing but fhade, and are not to compare with the harveft and fruits with which PEACE is crowned. He confiders that it is *nothing near fo meritorious to enlarge the limits of a kingdom a hundred leagues and more as to leffen our taxes twelve pence in the pound; and that there is lefs grandeur and real glory in defeating a hundred thoufand men than leaving twenty millions at their eafe and in fecurity.*

" Thus this mighty genius, who has been hitherto folely employed in contriving and raifing funds for the fupport of the war, in raifing recruits, taking cities, and gaining battles, will for the future wholly bufy himfelf in eftablifhing PEACE, WEALTH, and PLENTY. The fame head which brought forth a Pallas armed cap-a-pie, will fhow us the goddefs with her olive branch, peaceable, gentle, and learned, accompanied by all thofe arts which are generally to be found in her train. He will publifh no more new edicts but fuch as may tend to reftrain luxury and promote commerce. Those great vessels that were built to carry our arms beyond the Straits, shall for the future only bear our merchants and keep the seas open, and we shall have no more war but with the Algerines. Then the enemies of my Lord Cardinal will not be able to speak, as hitherto they have not been able to act, against him. Then the citizens of Paris shall be his guards, and he will be convinced how much more pleasing and satisfactory it is to hear his praises in the mouth of the people than in that of the poets. But I beseech you not to stand aloof till this happens, and stay not to be his Friend till you are forced to be so; but if you are resolved to persist in your opinion I shall not attempt to use any violence to dissuade you from it. However, be not so unjust as to take it ill that I have defended my own; and I freely promise you to read whatever you may think fit to write to me by way of answer, when the Spaniards have taken Corbie.—I am, Sir, your most obedient servant, Voiture."

It is to be wished that not only those of France and Germany, but all the European Powers, would carefully read and ponder the italicised paragraph in the foregoing letter. For civilization is a *fiasco*, and verbal Christianity an impious mockery, so long as nations from time to time continue to get up monster human shambles, call it "glory," inftead of what it *is*—gory, and thank Providence for the amount of wholefale murder; as if they ignored that great myfterious fact, that although, for fome infcrutable purpofe, God *permits* evil of every fort, yet He never *endorfes* it, even when it calls itfelf Victory. As for Napoleon III., no one of courfe in this enlightened age, is fo filly as to defend a dead lion. Given a ufurper, and of courfe you have that moft felf-feeking and unfcrupulous of all things — AMBITION. Still, the hollow, bitter world, with all its unlimited ingratitude, fhould not quite fo foon forget, and ftill lefs fhould the French forget, the two decades of plethoric profperity, European influence, and above all and more precious than all, the *order*, he beftowed upon France. As for, at this time of day, collecting cairns from which to lapidate the fallen Emperor's domeftic immorality, *that* is fuch a very pot-and-kettle proceeding for any one man to do to another, that it is doubly contemptible, from being both hypocritical and ridiculous. The very worft that can be faid of the ex-Emperor—for it includes all that is evil—is, that he graduated at GORE HOUSE —that cradle of all vice, and tomb of all virtue. It is to be hoped *that* emporium of focial, political, and literary turpitude, may never have **a** fucceffor.

"Dî talem terris avertite peftem!"

AN ESSAY UPON ESSAYS.

IF there be such a thing as sincerity in authors or truth in books, essay writing is unquestionably the truest and most sincere of any species of composition; for I take it that an essay is, as it were, the lining of at least one particular phase of the writer's mind, and consequently a modified reflex of the entire tone and calibre of his whole nature. But, as in the planetary system the sun is the original of the moon, so are there in the scheme of human intelligences solar minds, self-radiating in their own stupendous, inexhaustible, creative, and vivifying powers, and lunar minds, which reflect their rays, with great beauty and clearness, it is true, and with a certain influence upon the flux and reflux of events which form the tides of human opinions, but with no *universality* of power to penetrate into the most secret recesses of the innermost core of the great and many-pulsed heart of nature, like the omniprefent original luminary. For the fire, the facred fire, is the *foul* and centre of the one, and its mere calm, cold, fimulated reflex is the intellectual head-work of the other. Among thefe rare folar minds were thofe of Shakefpeare and Montaigne; the Univerfal was *in*, and emanated *from* both; while pre-eminent among the pale, cold, reflective, intellectual luminaries, were Lords Bacon and Shaftefbury. They might have written, but I doubt if either of them would have ever taken up the trade of THINKERS (for fuch it was with them), if Montaigne had not left them fuch an inexhauftible mine of original ore to work, and fuch ready excavated ingots to ftamp into popular currency. But here comes the great difference between the original luminary, with its glowing foul, that by one electric fpark carries yours on, and up, into the illimitable worlds of thought, and thofe mere cold, foullefs, reflected, intellectual lights, which indeed fhed a beauty and a charm upon even the moft ordinary and commonplace things, and fhow us clearly all that is to be feen in the phyfical world, making a fort of moral inventory for us of the property our mother Nature has bequeathed to us, and marking off thofe particular items that our ftepmother Fate will try to defraud us out of, but which from themfelves, poffeffing no vital warmth, cannot impart it, and from whofe catalogue of dry, hard, incontrovertible, unproductive, if not unsuggestive facts, we derive about as much pleasure and *real* good as we do when Suetonius informs posterity that Tiberius Cæsar's eyes were so luminous that he could see every object in the dark as clearly as by daylight, and that he had such auctioneer-hammer strength of knuckle that with one fillip of his fingers he could knock down a page and break his head into the bargain; which only proves what an admirable modern critic his imperial majesty would have made, being such an adept in the summary demolition of pages. And though very recondite and ingenious, the world has not derived any great benefit, or even an additional idea, from Hippocrates' account of the Macrocephali, or race of people with long heads—a race which indeed is still extant on the other side of the Tweed.

That "*rien n'est beau que le vrai*" is the *truest* truth that ever was uttered; and as light was sublimely said by Plato to be the "shadow of God," so is SIMPLICITY, the shadow or evidence of TRUTH, and the real test of greatness of mind. About the sham and the assumed there is always a glitter, a *faux brillant*, an *effort*, in fact, *de se faire valoir*, to *appear*, where to *be* is impossible. Monarchs wear diamonds, gold, and ermine, but the tinsel, cut glass, cotton velvet, and cat-skins of their mimic representatives on the stage, are of necessity lit up and set off with all sorts of false lights to dazzle the vulgar, and to *seem* like the reality for which they would fain pass. All this is the difference that ever has and ever will exist, between gilding and gold; but had there been no gold there would be no gilding, and this, like all other shadows,

" Proves the substance true."

The ambition to *attain* and to *appear*—that is, the angling for the opinions of men, with the semblance, or at least with the infinitesimal fragments, of virtues and estimable qualities, where, with half the same trouble we might in reality possess and practise them, is the infallible sign of an empiric, whether in an emperor, an author, a private individual, or a pseudo-philosopher. Now this straining after appearances and wishing to *seem* great, was especially the case with that " meanest of mankind" (and his brilliantly lacquered and gilded intellect) my Lord Verulam. As Tacitus says of Vespasian, he was *omnium quæ diceret aut ageret arte quadam ostentator;* that is, he had a certain art of setting off all he said or did, with a sort of ostentation; or like Corbulo, whom the same honest historian represents as *super experientiam sapientiamque etiam specie inanium validas,* namely, that besides his wisdom and experience, he made every trifling appearance become prevalent. Now, setting aside one's knowledge of the utter hollowness and corruption of Lord Bacon's character, but on the contrary, giving him the benefit of supposing that he fully acted up to the straight geometrical line of worldly probity and prudence that he inculcated in his writings, still it *is* but *worldly* straightforwardness and prudence, derived from the very narrowest, shallowest, and most mundane source; and you may read him forever by his own bright and perfectly well-trimmed patent lamp, and never feel the slightest love for or going out towards the man; your head unequivocally agrees with him, but your heart never communes with him for the best of all possible reasons—that he *has* no heart to commune with. Even the very fire he takes from the altar, in *his* hands is but a pale borrowed taper; for his religion (?) such as it was, was but an adoption of the last, and best, discovered lubricative for the STATE MACHINE—the decent and expedient covering for a cold heart and an attenuated soul. Incapable of love, he was equally impervious to friendship,[1] but the *theory* of the thing is of

---

[1] Such men as Lord Bacon have tools, flatterers, and what he himself would have called "followers;" but how could he (surcharged as he was with his own egotistical worldliness), possibly have felt friendship? For truly says Montaigne,

courſe to be reduced to proper worldly maxims, emanating from, revolving round, and reverting excluſively to SELF. And ſo he writes a tame, bald Eſſay "ON FOLLOWERS AND FRIENDS," and ſets out with the following highly-prudential axioms:—

"Coſtly followers are not to be liked, leſt, while a man maketh his train longer he maketh his wings ſhorter. I reckon to be coſtly, not them alone which charge the purſe, but which are weariſome and importune in ſutes [ſuits]; for ordinary followers ought to challenge no higher condition than countenance, recommendation, and protection from wrongs;"—with a great deal more of ſuch well-weighed, purely ſelfiſh, and one-ſided conſiderations, all of which might be ſummed up into the following apothegm:—

WITH REGARD TO THE WANTS, SORROWS, HOPES, FEARS, WRONGS, RIGHTS, FEELINGS, AFFECTIONS, OR WELFARE OF YOUR FELLOW CREATURES, INVARIABLY MAKE YOUR OWN IN- TERESTS THE FILTERING MACHINE.

How different is all this ſelf-worſhip and ſelf-

"Friendſhip is a ſacred thing, which can only ariſe between good men;—exiſts only by mutual eſteem; ſupports itſelf, not ſo much by ſervices on either part, as by goodneſs of life. That which makes one friend certain of another, is the knowledge that he has integrity; the ſureties which he has for him are his good diſpoſition, fidelity, and ſteadfaſtneſs."

patenting from dear old ſelf-forgetting and ſelf-abnegating Michel de Montaigne!¹ With a mind as immeaſurably beyond Lord Bacon's, as the Andes or Mount Olympus are above Primroſe Hill. It never enters into his wiſe, ſimple, honeſt head to be proud or vainglorious of the ſtupendous capacity God has given him; for inaſmuch as it *was* the gift of Omnipotence it appears to him as much a matter of courſe as his eyes, ears, hands, feet, or any other of the compound parts that make up the man called Michel Montaigne. The mind, the wondrous mind, he merely keeps well tended and cleared, as *the* light the ſame beneficent Creator has given him to guide him on his apointed way, and keep him in the right path. In his every act, in his

---

¹ Montaigne has been falſely called an egotiſt, becauſe he had ſo much ſincerity and ſo little vanity, as without reſerve to ſhow the ſhreds and croſs-grains of his mental hangings, as the obliging Gobeliners do of their tapeſtry to inquiſitive viſitors, after they have been charmed and inſtructed by the rich colouring and graphic epics produced by theſe curious ulterior workings. But egotiſm, properly ſo called, belongs to the odious moral, or rather groſſly immoral, attribute of ſelfiſhneſs. Of this moſt Stygian and polluting of all vices, the kind-hearted old Gaſcon gentleman's ever prompt and primary conſideration for others, whether his friends, his equals, his inferiors, or his ſuperiors, proved that he had not a particle. And as for the mere conſtant repetition of the pronoun "I," that is unavoidable in eſſay-writing, which is a ſort of phyſiographic autobiography.

every thought, without any flourish of trumpets in the way of professions or fine sentiments, you *feel* that he *knows* that the Moral, and not the Intellectual, is the lever of life—a lever whose fulcrum is in Eternity! His religion is neither a form, a sect, nor even a creed, so much as a deep, pure, subtile essence, a sort of angel leaven, which, while it causes his nature to rise above the earthly dross with which the best of human things are kneaded, at the same time curbs all his higher attributes into the most profound abnegation, the most unquestioning and child-like submission, to the Giver of those attributes; and even if he cannot suppress a smile at some of the nominal miracles of mediæval Italy, how quiet, how tolerant is that smile! for he knows that all such are but garbled legends of God's great concrete miracle of creation!

Never had a man, and still more a genius, so little of the *ego* in him. Whether he is giving a *festa di balla* and silk aprons and gauze head-dresses to the peasant girls at Della Villa (the baths of Lucca), taking a hint how cheaply he may improve his beds at Montaigne and those of the poor on his estate, or regretting he did not bring a cook with him that he might have picked up the knack of some of the quince soups and other nondescript *plats* he mentions,— all his wishes and actions have a spontaneous reference to the well-being or pleasure of others, and are jotted down in the same simple, truthful, unoftentatious way, with no fictitious motives assigned to them, and no finishing touches of either style or sentiment, so that they may appear to the more advantage in the Great Exhibition of publication. Then he honestly owns the badness of the Italian, in which his diary is written, for he has not the least wish or intention to impose the fiction on the public that he can write Italian as fluently and correctly as he does Latin or French, but only wrote in Italian, as he says, to exercise himself in that language, honestly regretting that during his tour he had associated too much with his own countrymen to make all the progress in the *lingua toscana* that he wished. My Lord Bacon would have either re-written it in Latin or choice Elizabethan English, put the bad Italian into the fire, or else have had it remodelled by some Roman *savant*, and so duly quartered with his own acquirements,—learning a cross, pretense, *fitchée*, humbug. I have always had a theory, and Montaigne confirms it, that the greatest minds are constructed upon the same principle as an elephant's trunk; that is, that while endowed with the strength and necessary power to raise and master the greatest things, they are at the same time gifted with a delicacy and minuteness of perception, for observing and picking up the smallest. And so we find Montaigne, on his journey through Germany, Switzerland, and Italy, quietly locking up the great laboratory of his mind, putting the key in his pocket, and with all the accuracy of the most perfect, thrifty, and notable housewife, observing and retaining the slightest novelty and improvement in domestic economy, were it only in the mode of airing linen, dressing a trout, or placing a saltcellar on a table; for he knew too much, not to know that it is of *little* things that that wondrous arcana that we call "life" is composed. There would be no globes if there were no globules. The analytic chemist is by far the subtlest. The most scientific workmen are employed for the minutest portions of watches and all other machinery. The finest lace, with its endless mob of bobbins and maze of almost invisible threads, is wrought by solitary women underground, lest the air should snap the threads (which are themselves like woven air, so impalpable,) and thus mar the design which is so beautiful, and though so complex, in its details, so simple in its effect, as a completed whole. Why then cannot the delicate threads attached to the clumsy and more ostensible bobbins of this great (and to our ignorant and uninitiated eyes) complicated lace pillow of creation remain in their places, and trust to the guidance of the skilful hand that knows how best to move them ? Why all this bother about "woman's miffion ? " Woman's miffion, like woman's fphere, is EVERYWHERE, though fhe has but ONE ORBIT, and that is, her HOME. True, fhe may, by the injuftice or brutality of man, be fhot from out that orbit, in its moft ftringent and conventional fenfe, and often have we caufe to regret in the prefent day,

> —— " that women, whofe price is fo far above rubies,
> Should fall to the lot of fuch brutes and fuch boobies ;"

but what then ? A true woman, like a bee, can find and hive fweets, and make a home anywhere, whether in a garden or in a defert. " Woman's miffion," like man's miffion, is *to do her duty in that ftate of life into which it has pleafed God to call her.* They may not, indeed, in many inftances have any witneffes to their fulfilment of this glorious miffion, or, as the cafe may be, martyrdom, befides that God who has appointed it; they may not even have the homœopathic *douceur*, the fmall Victoria medal, a biographer, to chronicle either their miffion or their martyrdom; for more Doctor Johnfons than are known, have lived and died, without a faithful Bozzy to make a double-entry of all the good things they faid and the better things they did; and whole circulating libraries of Mifs Brontës have been relieved from life's hard tread-

mill, without benefit of a Mrs. Gaſkell to perpetuate the manner in which they pealed potatoes
and the meritorious manner in which they did
not "eat mutton cold," but converted it into a
haſh for dinner. But neverthelefs, all and each
of thefe very important little things, which make
up their great account, *have* been duly entered,
depend upon it, in the imperiſhable Doomſday
Book above. Now don't let any woman who
does me the honour of reading thefe pages fuppofe for one moment that I am preaching up
the limited liability houfehold drudge fyftem for
women. God forbid! In a general way, it is
their ignorance that is their infirmity; the more
they know (mind, I don't fay that they *pretend*
to know, *or wiſh to be thought to know*), yes, the
more they know, the more they'll *do* and the
better they'll be. Some women, if in a garret, a
cellar, or more horrible than either, the cabin
of a ſhip! contrive to fill it with a happy and
HOME atmofphere, which is a fort of Claude glafs,
that beautifies the worft profpects into a pleafing
view. I knew an Englifh lady once, who, after
all her life being ufed to every luxury, was condemned to three fmall rooms in a continental
hotel. She was not exactly popular among her
compatriots. Who is poor in purfe, and not
equally poor in fpirit? Infolence, with money,
is independence; but independence of character

without money is pride.   Moreover, the misses
called her a "blue," becauſe ſhe was guilty of
knowing a little more than they did; the men,
becauſe ſhe was not a flirt nor a worſhipper of
their hereditary ſuperiority, proſcribed her as "a
ſtrong-minded woman," and

"Calomniez, calomniez!—il en reſte toujours quelquechoſe,"

as Scribe ſays; ſo I confeſs I was attacked with
the epidemic prejudice againſt her; for I do not
like blues, bores, or *ſo called* ſtrong-minded
women, any more than I like arſenic, ſtrychnine
or oxalic acid; only I have lived long enough to
know, that in this great drug mart, the world,
poiſons are often by miſtake labelled Simples, and
vice verſâ; but for one perſon who inveſtigates
the matter for himſelf, ten are poiſoned by
nominally innocent preparations, and twenty
avoid innocuous panaceas from their ſuppoſed
deleterious qualities, owing to the undeſerved
bad name beſtowed upon them.   But ſo it has
been ever ſince the world's dentition.   Our eyes,
which ſeldom deceive us, are rarely if ever con-
ſulted; while our ears, which have been filled
with falſehoods ever ſince his Satanic majeſty
was co-reſpondent in Paradiſe, are generally im-
plicitly believed.   Once, and once only, did I
hear anything like enthuſiaſtic praiſe beſtowed
upon this lady, and that was by a Frenchman,

who, upon hearing her duly diffected by a countrywoman of her own, fired up and faid—

" Non, non! elle eft charmante; à côté de l'efprit elle n'eft pas anglaife, et puis, c'eft la meilleure pâte de femme que la terre aît porté; elle fait du bien à tout le monde, d'autant plus, qu'elle *fait comment le faire.*"

And then, twirling his mouftache and turning to me, who fat next to him, he faid—

" Tenez, madame; je vous dirais deux mots charmants d'elle."

He then told me that one night, at Madame Récamier's, Châteaubriand had knocked down with his elbow a little Sèvre cup belonging to a *déjeuner.* He was in defpair at his awkwardnefs, but Madame Récamier made light of it, and faid it was of no confequence; whereupon Mrs. Greville, the Englifh lady in queftion, faid, turning to Châteaubriand—

" Ah, monfieur! on voit bien, que madame n'eft pas *Atala,* car elle ne met pas fon bonheur en chaque taffe! (*Chactas.*)"

" C'eft tres-joli, n'eft ce pas?" faid the Frenchman; to which I fully affented.

He then told me the other, which was, that he met Mrs. Greville at dinner one day at the Princefs L——'s. On going into dinner the fandal of her fhoe broke, and the Ruffian Prince,

G——, who was taking her in, seized it, and putting it into his waistcoat pocket, said—

"Ce petit brin de ruban sera le roman de ma vie!"

The hostess, hearing the word "roman," turned round and asked—

"De quel roman parlez vous, Prince?"

To which Mrs. Greville laughingly replied—

"Du dernier roman de Soulié, madame."

This was quite enough, and as the only thing I resolutely avoid is a fool, be it male or female, I resolved that I would call upon Mrs. Greville the next day. I did so, and after ascending the usual number of dirty stairs and encountering the *obligato* mosaic of atrocious odours indigenous to continental hotels,— of which that greatest of all abominations, stale tobacco smoke, is the *alpha* and *omega*—once within her rooms, the atmosphere was that of Arabia Felix; there was a delicate tepid perfume, floating, as it were, on the current of thorough fresh air that circulated freely through them. The first thing that struck you on entering was the appearance of intense and habitual comfort and the brilliant cleanliness. All the knickknackery was in such perfect order—the buhl blotting-books and desks polished as mirrors, the flowers so exquisitely arranged, the books looking what books ought to be—friends and companions, and not merely stuck up, doing company for the sake of their gorgeous bindings; so that every English person that came in exclaimed, " Oh ! what deliciously cosy, comfortable rooms !" and every foreigner, " *Ah ! comme c'est soignee ! comme tout cela a l'air grande dame !*" And yet poor Mrs. Greville had not even "a maid of her own !" and on that account, though so essentially and pre-eminently social, was obliged to relinquish going into society. But all this *bien-être* and elegant *entourage* were the daily work of her own hands. If you dined with her, though she never gave you but two things, they were perfect of their kind ; and there was no continental tagrag and deficits in the arrangements of the table—the glass, plate, and linen all having the same brilliant luxury of cleanliness ; for she had broken in one particular waiter and chambermaid to her ways. So true is it that some persons have the happy art, not only of *seeming* but of *being* more generous with sixpence than others can be with a hundred pounds ; because generosity consists in the feeling and the manner with which a thing is bestowed, and therefore is it, that the *obolus* of a really liberal nature, will always *win* more good will than a miser's thousands can *purchase*. When I knew Mrs. Greville more, I found out that I could have backed her against all the nurses of Scutari in a fick room, and that in the confection of a fhirt or a *falmi* fhe would have eclipfed the beft *chef* and fempftrefs extant; and although, added to all this, the woman *was* guilty of being able to argue with you from Ariftotle or expound to you from Epictetus, "pedantry" remained in her dictionary and was to be nowhere to be found in *her;* for I never knew a more thorough and *femi-ninely* feminine WOMAN in her habits and *ways,* and the depth and delicacy of her feelings; fo much fo, that no one would have ever fufpected that fhe was

> "learned, fave in gracious houfehold ways.
> Not perfect, nay, but full of tender wants;
> No angel; but a dearer being, all dipt
> In angel inftincts; breathing Paradife,
> Interpreter between the gods and men."

Withal generous and felf-facrificing, as *only* women *can* be, and what, had fhe been a man, would have been called "*the* beft fellow in the world!" But the alchemy of COMFORT in which fhe was fo pre-eminently fkilled, and which is one of the effential parts of "woman's miffion," arofe from her fcientific knowledge of and artiftic attention to detail, or *fmall things*—which are the *primum mobili* of all great ones. Archimedes moved the greateft weights by the fimple contrivance of three or four ordinary pieces of timber joined together, but the fecret confifted in the *order* and the art of their combination.

The greatest events in life, for good or evil, whether for nations or individuals, if traced to their source, will be generally found to have arisen from the *smallest*, and therefore apparently the most insignificant, causes. And truly says Cicero, in his fifth Philippic, *Quis nesciat minimis fieri momentis maximas temporis inclinationes?* namely, Who does not know that the greatest variations of time proceed from the minutest moments? Women, however, like Mrs. Greville, who *quietly* do their duty in that state of life into which it has pleased God to call them, ay, and do it even to the inanimate things about them, neglecting nothing, must resign themselves to living un*pronée* and dying unchronicled.

Que voulez vous? The greatest heroes are often born with a *valet de chambre* appended to them, and the greatest bores with a Bozzy. But courage, true-hearted women! Remember, that when Bethulia was to be delivered from the army of Holofernes, God did not employ mighty and steel-clad warriors, but He "*broke down their stateliness by the hands of a woman.*" What has been, may be again.

But to return to Montaigne. The greatest charm of the man to me is, his *reality*. He writes, *not* to gain a reputation, nor even to assume the superiority of teaching his fellow-men, but because the deep well-spring of thought is *there*, and muſt guſh out ; and *that*, conſidering the perilous and bigoted times in which he wrote, with a pure, undefiled, and fearleſs honeſty, is beyond all praiſe. And this genuineneſs and guileleſs ſimplicity pervaded his whole character. For in his journal, when he ſpeaks of the ovations he received in his travels, it is always with a little innocent ſort of humble vanity, as if he thought it *ſo* good and kind of the people ; and never dreamt of arrogating any compliment as a juſt debt to his own merits ; ſo that one can almoſt fancy one ſees the reflection of his half pleaſurable half modeſt bluſh on the paper when he adds, " But no doubt it is their cuſtom to offer theſe courteſies to all ſtrangers of a certain rank." Of the immeaſurable ſuperiority in calibre, depth, breadth, and originality of Montaigne's mind over Lord Bacon's there can be no doubt ; and as far as mere learning goes, which is not intellect, but merely the food of intellect, there is a greater and deeper ſource of it in *one* of Montaigne's eſſays, to ſay nothing of the pith and marrow of *true* wiſdom, than in all Lord Bacon ever wrote. Like the golden thigh of Pythagoras, mentioned by Diogenes Laertius, but which Plutarch tells us in his life of Numa was a mere charlatanic ſtratagem of the philoſopher's [!] to convey to his admirers and the vulgar, (who conſtitute the ballaſt of all artificial celebrity,) an impreffion of his divinity, fo my Lord Bacon, if duly weighed in the fcales of impartiality, will be found to have given us more golden thigh than golden rules.

To gauge the minds of the two men, it is only neceffary to recall Lord Bacon's Capel-Court-Minories maxims,—how to avoid rifking our own welfare, intereft, or comfort in any way for our friends, and how always to make ufe of them without giving them any chance of returning the compliment (*here*, at all events, the great man, the peripatetic of the golden thigh, *practifed* what he preached!)—you have only, I fay, to recall thefe crooked, hard, worldly maxims, and compare them with Montaigne's friendfhip for and devotion to, the memory of Monfieur de la Boëtie. There is nothing on record more true, more perfect, or more beautiful, than the former, or more tender, touching, and conftant, than the latter. The truly great are thofe, not whofe writings make us wifer in the world's fhallow lore, but thofe whofe lives make us better. Great, then, is the debt that the world owes to thee, oh! MICHEL DE MONTAIGNE! for after a life fpent in life's beft humanities and kindlieft links, who ever left a lovelier example, not fo much of the ruling paffion as of the ruling virtue "ftrong in death" as thou didft? For we are told that fhortly before his death, his tongue becoming paralyzed, he could not speak; so writing down to have all his servants called in, he got out of bed, put on his dressing-gown, and when they were assembled *gave* them each with his own dying hands, the legacies he had left them, fearing that when he was dead, they might be put to inconvenience, trouble, or expense to obtain them. Ten minutes after he had conferred this, his last, act of considerate kindness upon them, he expired.

Verily this was better, nobler, greater, than the vain-glorious, arrogant, and therefore somewhat ludicrous pomposity of a man's bequeathing his own fame to the world, and after a time, to his country; for it was leaving his whole nature — that inalienable personal estate — to ETERNITY, and APPOINTING OMNIPOTENCE AND THE RECORDING ANGEL AS HIS EXECUTORS! The fruit and foliage are the visible, and sought-after portions of a tree, but its and their vitality is in the roots; and the *morale* is the root of humanity. It is for this reason that the merely intellectual, however transcendent, is but an air-plant, that has no radical source of duration. Thus the world outgrows its Mirabeaus, Bolingbrokes, Humes, Gibbons, and Voltaires, which are but so much head-gear, the fashion of which changeth and passeth away; but the world, or rather human nature, never outgrows its Shakespeares, Senecas, and Montaignes; becaufe fuch minds are the pulfes and arteries of its great univerfal heart. Goethe, if we take the mere meafure of his brain, was of larger calibre than Schiller; but the moral organization of the MAN, being cold, fhallow, and defective, dies with his body, and finds no embalming procefs in the hearts of his fellow-men, as Schiller did, when once his light had gone out. For pofterity is juft; and it is always THE WHOLE MAN, and not the mere brain, that it diffects. Therefore, all honour to *thee*, now and evermore, wife, good, fubtle yet fimple, profound, clear-minded, nice-confcienced, broad-hearted, MICHEL DE MON-TAIGNE!

AN OLD MAN'S SAYING.

HAD once a grandfather; indeed I believe the thing is *not* uncommon, though it is the fafhion to fay that fome perfons never had one. Be that as it may, I'm fure no one ever had fuch a dear old lovable grandfather as mine was. I'm not going to fentimentalize over him. Heaven forbid that I fhould fo mock the manes of the nobleft nature and trueft heart that ever iffued from the Maker's mint, and which, when called in, returned to it, with the Sovereign's likenefs and fuperfcription in no way defaced or corroded by their long currency among men. No, I'm not going to fentimentalize over him, for *he* was no fentimentalift,—fortunately for himfelf, and more fortunately ftill, for thofe belonging to him. For your profeffed fentimentalift is generally a finifhed fcoundrel, or at beft a frothy theorift, totally devoid of affections and principles.

Befides, about fentimentalifts as about all other charlatans and pretenders, there is generally a fpice of pompofity, and my grandfather had not an atom of that Bœotian buckram about him. His manners (the moft finifhed of the old fchool, which *had much* artiftic finifh about it,) were far too bland, eafy, polifhed, and high bred, to have the flighteft taint of the *parvenu* rigidity of pompofity in them. It was not on account of his being the hero of a hundred fights, his having conducted feveral embaffies and miffions to a fuccefsful iffue, or the broad ribbon of the Bath that glowed acrofs his ample cheft, the ftars of half the European orders that formed a galaxy on his breaft, the freedoms of cities in their gold boxes, the fable peliffes and the diamond fnuff-boxes he poffeffed in fufficient number to have put away each of his own virtues feparately in, nor even his brilliant and truly claffical wit, that lightened in his eyes before it flafhed from his lips, which ftamped him fo unmiftakably for what he was—A THOROUGH GENTLEMAN, but the genuine, genial, and practical Chriftianity of his whole life, that made him the idol of thofe two juftly judging extremes—YOUTH and AGE.

Many men have not only a fine outline but an amiable quality of character; but they lack the minute Flemifh painting of detail, the womanly anticipatory kindnefs of *little* things, the gentle glidings of true unfelfifh goodnefs, which is feen and *felt,* but is too noifelefs to be ever *heard.* And thefe my grandfather had, more even than any *woman* I have ever known. He did not hang up his cremona behind the door at home, like many other celebrated performers in the *rôle* of *beaux efprits* in fociety, but with an inexhauft-ible fund of anecdote, chiefly gleaned from his own ftirring and eventful life, had always the *mot pour rire;* he was juft as racy, brilliant, and agreeable *en petit comité,* with us children on a fummer lawn, or by a winter firefide, as he would have been among all the magnates of the land. For he was at once a realization and an incarna-tion of Bifhop Hall's axiom, that "Love and action do neceffarily evince each other. True love cannot lurk long unexpreffed: it will be looking out at the eyes, creeping out of the mouth, breaking out at the finger's ends, in fome actions of dearnefs; efpecially thofe wherein there is pain and difficulty to the agent, profit or pleafure to the affected. O Lord, in vain fhall we profefs to love Thee if we do nothing for Thee! Since our goodnefs cannot reach up unto Thee, who art our glorious head, O let us beftow on Thy feet (Thy poor members here below,) our tears, our hands, our ointment, and whatever other gifts or endeavours may teftify our thankfulnefs and love to Thee in them."

With the moft joyous and genial nature, that diffufed itfelf like funfhine over all around him, yet, in the great fellowfhip of human forrow and human fuffering, was he ever foremoft. His firft *thought* was always how he could either ferve, fave, or give pleafure; and, as in fire-arms, the report follows the flafh, fo in his moral arfenal the deed ever followed quick upon the thought. Truly his whole life was a redemptive conflict to a glorious and eternal victory! For fhall not thofe who fuffer for, and with their fellow pilgrims, and thus ferve their God as He has ordained here, reign with Him hereafter? Yea, verily, as furely as yon golden fun that fets today fhall rife again in glory to-morrow!

Dear old man! not only is thy fhadow lefs on this bleak cold earth now, but few other fubftances are there, worthy to replace even that beneficent fhadow which never *darkened* any threfhold; but with a holier and more tempered light, fuch as an angel's wing might do, laden with glad tidings.

But heaven knows beft; let none difpute it. My grandfather lived and died juft as, and when he ought. He could never have got on in the prefent day at all. The ticket-of-leave fyftem of politics alone, would have driven him mad; for he had fpoken in Parliament when oratory was the *thing*, not the *word*; and patriotifm was deemed a *fine quâ non* for its foundation ; and when *his* voice woke the fenate, he had had Europe for an echo, and Edmund Burke for an auditor and a panegyrift. Neither am I at all fure that the literature, or rather the *literati*, of the prefent day would have fuited him ; for, as he was fully capable of appreciating the improvement in the *former*, and the degeneration in the latter, he would have been continually deploring, that where fuch an immenfe floating capital of undeniable talent of a very high order exifts, the owners of it had not the fame advantage as that attributed to Terence by an old writer, who, in fpeaking of the graphic and vividly life-like delineations of character and the unctuous humour of his come-dies, thinks that his chief merit was owing to his having had the good fortune to have Scipio and Lælius to give his *dramatis perfonæ* " the true turn of gentlemen."

But above all, this prefent time would not have fuited my grandfather, nay, it would have been pofitively antipathetic and antagoniftic, to him, from its being a utilitarian age, that generally walks, no matter how dirty the ways, moftly in highlows, and *always* with its breeches pockets clofely buttoned. It never *fays* either a foolifh or a rude thing, but it alfo never *does* a kind or a civil one. It goes about giving lec-tures to the great unwafhed, for it is an old and a true faying, that words coft nothing; whereas the fmalleft modicum of foap (with the exception of foft-foap), would neceffitate at leaft fome trifling globule of pecuniary outlay. It takes up ftarving wretches for prefuming to beg, but it never begs any meafure to prevent them ftarving. It builds, Bibles, miffions, magnifies, preaches, and *profeffes* Chriftianity; in fhort, does everything but *practife* it. Our philanthropy, which, like our preferves, *ufed* to be confected at home, is now all done abroad, in joint-ftock, companies, limited (and *very* limited too), *via* ragged fchools, penitentiaries, fhoeblack brigades, anything and everything that can enable us to buy our benevolence in the cheapeft market, and blazon it in the deareft. But to hope for one *individual* touch of fympathy, or even common humanity, from thefe wholefale charity-mongers, would indeed be like the futile tafk of attempting to extract funbeams from cucumbers, as a fingle ftiver from thefe profeffional Samaritans' [?] *own* coffers is never forthcoming. On *principle,* they never do anything of the kind; for this is a commercial country, where *intereft* and principal are very properly infeparable; and unknown, anonymous individual fympathy (that had not been organized into a committee, or incorporated in a fat commiffionerfhip), would be *interfering in private affairs;* and beftowing a fixpence that did not flow from the tributary ſtreams of public contribution, would be encouraging idleneſs and vagabondiſm, and is ſhocking, immoral, and not to be thought of—and ſo it never *is* thought of.

Alas for my poor primitive, unphiloſophical, and monetarily immoral grandfather! though he did ſubſcribe largely, to all the hoſpitals and public charities, yet there were, as there ſtill are and ever will be, ſo many ſharp, keen, yet ſhamefaced neceſſities, that never come within the pale of public munificence, ſuch myriads whoſe rags have been *once* fine linen, who cannot dig, and who to beg are aſhamed, that ſomehow or another my grandfather's hand was never out of his own pocket; but what it took from thence, ſo far as its owner was concerned, always remained a myſtery between himſelf and the God in whoſe ſervice he beſtowed it, and although

" Open as day to melting charity,"

that ſaid right hand of his, was the only cloſe ſecretive thing about him; for I verily believe its ſiſter hand quitted *this* world, in total ignorance of the ſplendid collection of light hearts and bright faces, it had ſo laviſhly bought; till their final account was audited in the next. But the gifts of that hand (and a beautiful one it was, by-the-by, as if to bleſs and to give were all it had been created for, and that, confequently, it had done naught elfe), unftrained as thefe gifts were, they were but the fpray and fprinklings, from that inexhauftible fountain, his pure, deep, illimitable heart. When I look· back upon the quiet beauty of that old man's life, I envy him not fo much even for all the good he did, as for the *way* in which he did it, he fo thoroughly underftood the art; but then, to be fure, it was his whole ftudy. If it were only to buy a toy for a child, or a trinket for a young girl, he always took the pains to fift out the identical toy or trinket that was moft wifhed for; and any affair he undertook for others, however intricate, tedious, or even hopelefs, he was not fatisfied to wait till fome tangible bufinefs point had been achieved, to communicate with thofe for whom he had undertaken it; for, as he himfelf was wont to fay, all bufinefs is flow, but fufpenfe is feverifh and wayward; and moreover, to thofe who fuffer and hope, and ftill more, to thofe who fuffer and fear; minutes feem hours, hours days, days weeks, weeks months, and months years; and fo he filled up the great defolate fpace between expectation and fruition, with kind words of fympathy and hope. This would have been *real* goodnefs, even had he been an idle man, with a large furplus of golden leifure to fpend as he pleafed; but he

was not, for, although an habitually and confti-
tutionally early rifer, every minute of his twelve
hours had its appointed work ; and though I
have often heard him complain of not having
had time to anfwer the letters of very great per-
fonages as immediately as his nice punctilio of
good breeding deemed right, yet I never knew
him not to *make* time, to anfwer, or to take the
initiative in writing to, thofe who were in any
way diftreffed " in mind, body, or eftate;" fo that
it was a high compliment (and we felt it and
meant it as fuch) when my coufins and fifters
and myfelf faid his dear, honeft, noble, handfome
old head reminded us of Nep's. Nep, or Nep-
tune, was a big Newfoundland dog, at once our
idol and our victim, and the " guide, companion,
friend," of the whole family. Only Nep's handfome head was black, with merely a white mark
up his forehead, that we ufed to call a falt-fpoon ;
and my grandfather, continuing the fafhion of
his day, wore powder ; but it was the fweeteft of
all violet powder, with a fubftratum of peculiarly
fragrant jeffamine pomatum, which Pendrel, his
old valet, who had been with him in all his
campaigns, would have thought facrilege to have
got anywhere but where he had got it for forty
years,—at Smith's, in Bond Street. Never to this
day does a foft breath of violets and jeffamine
figh through the air, without bringing the tears

to my eyes, and all my youth back to me, with its long funny viftas, and that dear old grandfather, and Nep, my mother, coufins, fifters, all! peopling them as vividly as of old. Such magical and myftical "open fefames" of memory's moft fecret cells, are the "linkèd fweetnefs" of both mufic and perfumes!

But tufh! there is no ufe in my going back all this way to meet thofe who never can return to meet me here. Would that I could hope to be worthy of meeting them hereafter! And yet, were juftice alone to gauge God's goodnefs, dare the beft amongft us hope? But between the twin feraphs—Mercy and Faith—the worft need not defpair.

When I began this paper I merely intended to have recorded one faying of my grandfather's, but truly, "Out of the fullnefs of the heart the mouth fpeaketh." So now let me make up for loft time, by recording that golden faying, or, I fhould rather fay, rule, of his,—which I have never forgotten; and may all who read it here never do fo either!—which is one of the beft wifhes I can offer them.

It was on a gufty evening in September, we were at Richmond, in one of thofe pleafant houfes clofe to the Park. There were no railways in thofe days, but admirable pofting (worth them all, except for fpeed), and long ftages and ſhort ſtages, and mail coaches, and pack-horſes, and canal-boats, *et voilà tout*, and no penny poſtage, ſo the twopenny poſt was thought a great deal of, and conſidered one of the greateſt boons and improvements of modern times. It was, as I before ſaid, a guſty evening in September, and we children, with the deſſert (for there were no *dîners à la ruſſe* in thoſe days), had juſt made our appearance. Now, if my grandfather *had* a fault, it was that he was a bit of a coddle; but no ; it was not a fault, it was an averſion, that he ſhared in common with all old people, to draughts, night air, and moving immediately after dinner. Juſt before dinner, he had deſpatched couſin Robert, Meg, and me, in preference to a ſervant, with a note to a poor gentleman of the name of Trevor, a half-pay captain, who, with a wife and four children, was lodging over a bookſeller's ſhop in the town. I ſuſpect the note contained a ſomewhat more flimſy incloſure, for my grandfather always wrote upon very thick-ribbed wove paper, and uſed envelopes, which at that time nobody elſe did, except, perhaps, old Lord Hertford, the Prince Regent, and the perſons immediately about him. Not that for a moment I mean to claſs theſe with nobodies,— their phyſical greatneſs alone, and the immenſity of evil they did in their generation (which we in ours are now paying for), would preclude my doing fo. And fo, from the thicknefs of the paper, I could not be fure about the inclofure, for Robert had orders to fend it up by the fervant and wait in the fhop for the anfwer, that he might not in any way intrude on the Trevors. But from the tears that were in the poor gentleman's eyes when he himfelf brought us down the anfwer, I long after fufpected that there was an inclofure,—for at the time, child-like, I thought nothing about it. Juft as we returned with the captain's miffive the letters *via* the evening's poft were brought in, and amongft them was a long official document, "O.H.M.S.," with a large War Office feal on it. My grandfather, who was in the act of raifing a glafs of wine to his lips, put it down, and haftily broke the feal of the long blue parallelogram.

"Come! that's capital!" he exclaimed. "Bring me my hat, great coat, and gloves," faid he to the butler, from whom he had juft taken the letters, as the latter was about to leave the room.

"Surely, my dear father," faid my mother, "you are not going out! more efpecially on foot?"

"Tut, tut! that am I," rejoined my grandfather, rifing as he fpoke.

"I can tell you it's blowing what you call great guns, fir," put in Robert, longing to begin upon the walnuts without incurring the delay of any exodus.

"Why, my dear child," faid my grandfather, addreffing my mother, "I muft go, to give poor Trevor the good news before it cools and he fees it firft in the *Gazette* to-morrow. Fancy! the poor fellow has got his majority, and the appointment at Corfu alfo; fo now he'll do!"

"I'm very glad of it; but furely a fervant can go? or Robert will go again," remonftrated my mother.

"No, no; I would not mifs the fellow's face when he hears of it," faid my grandfather, "for a Field-marfhal's baton! For *I* never held out any hopes to him, and *he* was *quite fure he* never fhould get either his promotion or the appointment."

And this was faid with a long face, a fhake of the head, and a deep figh, in ludicrous imitation of poor Captain Trevor, which fet all of us children laughing.

"Well, but grandpapa," faid I, "you can go and tell him to-morrow morning."

"Child!" he cried, turning fharply round, and laying his hand with fome force on my fhoulder, fo as to imprefs his words, as it were, "you are a good girl enough, in your way, and though not likely ever to injure your health by too clofely poring over your books," (I was then twelve), "yet, I fuppofe you know what the copybook fays, that 'PROCRASTINATION IS THE

THIEF OF TIME?' Well, *I* tell you that it's *worfe*, for it is often the MURDERER both of opportunity and of thofe whofe hopes and lives hang upon very flender threads. So remember, my child, if you wifh to be all *en régle*, and have your paffport properly *vifé* for your final journey, for which none of us know how foon the *route* may come—

"NEVER PUT OFF TILL TO-MORROW THE MAKING A SAD HEART GLAD, IF IT CAN BE DONE TO-NIGHT."

SERVANTS.

ICERO relates that the ugliest and most stupid slaves in Rome came from England. Moreover, he urges his friend Atticus *not* to bring slaves from Britain, on account of their stupidity, and their inaptitude to learn music and other accomplishments. Cæsar also describes the Britons as a nation of very barbarous manners. In another place he remarks, "In their domestic and social habits the Britons are regarded as the most savage of all nations."

> "But, pray, young England, don't your sires despise,
> For just *such, you* seem, to many modern eyes."

And so, my young friends, you are likely to appear in the eyes of Europe, till each individual Briton can resolutely resolve to shuffle off his national arrogance and self-sufficiency, and strenuously apply himself to *individual reform;* for believe me, manners, next to morals, are the moſt important ingredient in the great ſocial *olla podrida*, and like hard eggs in a *mayonnaiſe*, unleſs they be blandly blent with the other nominally more important items, but mar them all by *their* ſingle failure. And general rules and wholeſale ſyſtems never will achieve this equal and moſt deſirable amalgamation, for each ſeparate adjunct requires a ſpecial and individual caſe. You want morally, what Herodotus tells us the Egyptians had phyſically: "Each phyſician," he ſays, "applies himſelf to ONE diſeaſe only, and no more. But all places abound in phyſicians; ſome are for the eyes, others for the head, others for the teeth, others for internal diſorders." And it is impoſſible to mix with any grade of Engliſh ſociety, without feeling how much, how very much, the MANNERS DOCTOR is needed for the community at large; for every one, with the few and rare exceptions that prove the rule, ſprouts his or her own thiſtle, and alas! *Non inultus premor.*

And this being the only thing *piquante* about the ſaid ſociety, unfortunately does not render it the more agreeable. And moſt decidedly, no claſs requires the MANNERS, and above all, the MORALS DOCTOR, ſo much as the ſervants—or rather, the no-ſervants of the preſent day—who poſſeſs in a pre-eminent degree all the diſqualifications attributed by Cicero to their anceſtors; the ſlavery only entirely left out, as they are much more nearly related to a certain Cuffy upon an American planter's eſtate, previous to the abolition of the infernal inſtitution of ſlavery (that is, of chartered ſlavery, for *un*chartered ſlavery, it is to be feared, will, like "the poor," never ceaſe from the earth). Well, Mr. Cuffy, that typical " nigger," upon being remonſtrated with by his owner, calling him " A lazy raſcal, who was afraid of work," replied with equal truth and ſimplicity, " Me not afraid of work, maſſa; me lie down and go to ſleep beſide him." But theſe modern Engliſh ſemidetached Cuffies, the preſent race of ſervants, do more than this, for they have a noble contempt for work, and neglect it altogether; always, like the Levite in the parable, " paſſing by, on the other ſide." There can be no doubt that the power of disfiguring paper with ink, and, as if ſtung into revenge by all the " ſpelling bees," making a raid upon orthography, ſupplemented by the power of reading all their maſters' and miſtreſſes' letters, and enabling " Lizer" to incite " Sarer Jane," *via* the penny poſt, to additional malpractices and inſubordination, miſnomered "education," which has been beſtowed upon it, has a great deal to anſwer for, " a *little* learning" being proverbially a dangerous thing, whether derived from the *Pierian* or the parifh fpring. But the chief "origin of evil," fo far as the female clafs of domeftic fervants is concerned, is the want of thofe admirable vanity safety-valves, fumptuary laws, which would provide and enforce a neat, decent, and becoming coftume for them, and prevent their exaggerating what is already a hybrid between a nightmare and a caricature, *i.e.* each fucceeding hideous fafhion, the prefent moft unbecoming and indecent *fortir du bain* ftyle of dreffes having caufed even a new Shakefpearean reading, which fays:—

> "There is a tide in the affairs of men,
> And a *tied back* in the affairs of women!"

For drefs, however ugly, trumpery, and disfiguring, is always *coftly* to every clafs, according to its means, or *want of means*, for indulging in it. And the high prieft which enables the "fervant gal" clafs to facrifice to this Moloch is, DISHONESTY; for there are a hundred ways of being difhoneft, without reforting to the ftraightforward and perilous one of putting hands into other perfons' pockets, or abftracting bank notes from their defks or *efcritoires;* fuch, for inftance, as making their employers pay toll upon everything that comes into their houfes; purchafing, both in food and all other articles, the cheapeft refuſe, and charging the higheſt price aſked for the beſt things; in ſhort, ſtrictly carrying out the late Sir Robert Peel's commercial axiom, a very ſuper-erogatory one, ſo far as England is concerned, of "always buying in the cheapeſt and ſelling in the deareſt market." But the very worſt, and to their employers moſt ruinous, to their maſters and miſtreſſes, or rather as things now are, to their ſlaves and dependents, is, their want of knowing *how* to do the commoneſt things, either in the ſhape of houſehold or needle work, in the firſt place, and their idleneſs in the next, as they live on and for excitement alone, *via* conſtant "outing" and excurſion trains. Their worſt and moſt ruinous diſhoneſty, I maintain, ariſes from their total neglect; which cauſes everything entruſted to them, whether plate, glaſs, china, linen, books, or furniture, to go to deſtruction. But all this, fills their exchequer for the three or four months they condeſcend to ſtay in a place, and *via* the ſaid trumpery dreſs and the eternal excurſions, to provide their *one* aim in life, a "young man," whom they literally "pick up" and marry, without a farthing in their pockets or the moſt latent power of earning one in their head, or hands, or habits, ſo as to make anything like a *home* for themſelves or the "young man." And hence all the horrible and ſummary wife-murders, from drink and deſperation, cauſed by

dirt, diforder, and domeftic difcomfort. Formerly, no one would think of taking a fervant
who had lived *only* fix months in a place; now,
that is thought a long term; and as to a character from their laft place, they are quite inde-
pendent of *that*, either by falfe ones, or through
thofe focial pefts, called "fervants' regiftry
offices," whofe fole *raifon d'être* is to fleece both
the hirer and the hired, and who know nor care
nothing for either.   Formerly, fervants had at
leaft, good, honeft, induftrious mothers, who
before their daughters ever attempted to go to
fervice, taught them their place, if they could
not teach them their bufinefs; and above
all, took care to inculcate the golden rule of
"fubmitting to thofe in authority over them,"
and alfo habits of thrift, with fufficient induftrial
knowledge to enable them to make and mend,
their own clothes.   Now, thanks to fewing
machines, and other royal roads to idlenefs, they
do not know how to thread a needle, much lefs
how to ufe one; and afk the rector or curate
of any parifh, and he will tell you the fame
ftory; with variations, it may be, but the motive
is invariably the fame, *i.e.*, that if he give to
the mother of an almoft ftarving family half-a-
crown of a Saturday evening, it is *not* food it
will be transformed into, but fome coarfe imitation of a flower, or a rat's-tail of a feather for

the eldeſt girl's hat, to enable her to look additionally vulgar and diſreputable on the following
day at church. Naturally, *je prêche pour ma
paroiſſe ;* for having for thirty years had the
good old thorough-bred, well trained, efficient,
truſtworthy, devoted ſervants, overflowing with
gratitude for what was *leſs* than their due, and
who lived with me till they died, the preſent
extreme of incapacity, vulgar inſubordination,
and black ingratitude, was really too great a
ſhock to ſoul, nerves, and body. Formerly,
when I eulogized, as in common juſtice I never
was tired of doing, the good qualities and devotion of my ſervants, I was met with, " Oh, no
wonder you have good, truſtworthy, and devoted ſervants ; ſee how kind and how liberal
you are to them." Now, when I complain of
their incapacity, inſubordination, and the not
being able to humaniſe, much leſs to buy them
at any price, the anſwer is, " No wonder ; you
ſpoil, and are too generous and too indulgent to
them, and the common Engliſh nature never
underſtands that ſort of thing, more eſpecially as
they don't meet with it elſewhere, and ſo they
only take advantage of you in every way they
can, thinking it is folly, and not kindneſs, which
makes you act in ſo exceptional a manner."

This *is* verifying Prior's lines with a ven-
geance !—

> "Gently touch and smooth a nettle,
> It will sting you for your pains;
> Use it rough, as man of mettle,
> And it soft as silk remains.
> 'Tis the same with vulgar natures—
> Treat them kindly, they rebel;
> Use them rough as nutmeg-graters,
> *Then* the rogues will treat you well."

But, considering that so many of the *soi-disant* ladies (?) of "the period" have adopted the language of servants and all the verbal kitchen exotics, it is not much to be wondered at that the tone of their minds should, as a natural sequence, sink to the same calibre; for when one hears what, according to their social position, should be gentlewomen, say to a servant, "Tell *Cook* I shall dine at seven," or, "Tell *Coachman* I want the carriage at two;" or when they ring the bell, say, "Coals, *please*," or "Tea, *please*," and call going in a carriage or cab "*riding*," or call needle-work by the generic term of "sewing," or perfume by the intensely vulgar and peculiarly servant's-hall name of "scent," it is not, verily, much to be wondered at, that, in hiring a servant for a friend, by way of courting popularity with the very low upstarts who now call themselves servants, instead of impressing their duties upon the nominal servant, they should lower their *soi-disant* friend in every possible way, by saying, "This lady is very fidgetty,"—the kitchen term for any miftrefs who exacts order and obedience in her houfe,—" But *you* muft *put up* with that, and I'm fure you'll find it a good place upon the whole."　One of thefe "ladies" with the minds of laundreffes, having got a cook for a friend, which cook turned out a confirmed drunkard and thief—which was no poffible fault of the lady who hired her, but only her misfortune, juft as, if fhe had turned out perfection, it could have been no merit of this lady's, but merely a fortunate coincidence—yet, when another friend tried her hand, and got for her friend another cook, who turned out a worfe thief and drunkard than the former one, inftead of expreffing any fympathy or commiferation to her friend for her continued trouble and difappointment, the high-minded and amiable view the firft lady took of her friend's uncomfortable pofition was to rub her hands and fay, "Ah! I'm glad others cannot fucceed any better than I did!"　Verily "Lizer" or "Sarer Jane" could not have faid more!—though even *they* might have faid lefs.

Next comes the exceeding ftuckupativenefs[1] of thefe ftarving waifs and ftrays from cellars, gar-

---

[1] A lady, a few evenings ago, fpeaking upon this peculiar phafe of the "fervant gal" craze upon "the genteel," in which they even furpafs Mr. Towle, told an amufing anecdote of the letter-bag being opened one day at breakfaft, and, among the other contents, was a letter on pink paper, directed "To Mifs

rets, and back lanes. They are too fine to carry a parcel, were it only the fize of a penny roll, and did the fate of an empire depend upon having it immediately, and no matter how great the lofs to their employers. Of courfe it was not *their* fault; for they are all popes as to infallibility, and kings that can do no wrong. They ordered it, and the tradefpeople promifed to fend it directly; fo what more could *they*, the fervants, do?

This reminds me of two ftories. One a friend of mine told me whofe grandfather was Bifhop of ———. She faid, going through the hall one day, he heard a tremendous fquabbling, and very loud excited voices in the lower regions; and upon inquiring the caufe of the butler, who had juft announced that the carriage was at the door, he was told that fomething was wrong with the oven; and the cook having ordered Bridget the kitchen-maid to take a certain venifon pafty, that could not be baked at home, to the baker's, that young lady had flatly refufed to walk through the ftreets fo encumbered. Whereupon, the bifhop ordered both the delinquent and the pafty, to come to him. Then, telling the carriage to wait till his return, he marched the blufhing Bridget in Indian

Jemima Jenkins, Efqr." (!) This turned out to be for the kitchen-maid; feeing her mafter's letters fo directed, no doubt fhe had informed her correfpondent that this was the "*genteel* thing to do," and exacted this tribute to her focial ftatus.

file before him, took the pasty himself, and carried it in great state to the baker's, as if he had been walking at a coronation, with the crown on a velvet cushion. The legend further tells, that Bridget never again refused to carry pasties or anything else to the baker's, and even carried *herself* in a much more becoming manner ever after.

The other story is better known, being of Rowland Hill, who told his coachman to go every morning to a farmhouse, at about a mile's distance, for the milk and cream for breakfast. Whereupon that functionary refused, with much offended dignity, saying that that was not *his* business to do. "Oh, I beg your pardon," said Rowland Hill; "then may I ask, what you do strictly consider your business?"

"Why, to drive the carriage, sir."

"Oh, very well! Then have it at the door every morning at half-past six punctually; and drive Mary the housemaid to —— farm for the cream."

Formerly no girl thought of going to service until she had learnt at least the rudiments of household work from her mother, which even the poorest mother, in those days, was capable of teaching. Now, they issue ready dressed out, from their cellars, garrets, or back lanes, knowing *literally* nothing, and quite determined they won't be taught any thing, and think it "very *ard* they are told so often the same thing;" but it never enters their heads to think it at all hard for their miſtreſs to have to tell them the ſame thing ſo often. When I firſt married, it was one of my ways of trying to ſerve my fellow creatures, to take girls out of the village when in the country, and have them thoroughly well trained under the houſekeeper in all the uſages of houſehold work, and what is equally eſſential, taught the quiet, reſpectful manners of a ſervant; and *then*, but not till then, they ſought a place, aſking but little wages at their firſt ſituation, and gradually aſking more as they improved in capability and deſerved more. Now, every dreſſed-out ſlattern, who has never lived in ſervice before, and is conſequently obliged to own that ſhe knows nothing of houſe-hold work, but modeſtly adds ſhe has no doubt ſhe can do it all if ſhe tries, begins by aſking, or rather demanding, £20 a year;[1] which *uſed* to be the wages one gave one's own maid, ſkilled in dreſs-making, hair-dreſſing, and all the other duties belonging to her department. The pre-

---

[1] Now though it is unfortunately quite true that houſe rent, taxes, and every ſpecies of food, groceries excepted, are three times as dear as they were twenty, and twice as dear as they were ten years ago, yet the only two things upon which maid-ſervants ſpend their money, namely, trumpery dreſs, and excurſion trains, on the other hand, are twice as cheap as they were at either of the above-named periods; ſo that there is no valid reaſon, or even plauſible pretext, why their wages ſhould have increaſed ſo prepoſterouſly.

fent houfemaidenly *débutantes* alfo lofe no time in ftating moft ftringently and fpecifically, *their* requirements as to hours of rifing, going to bed, and their Sundays out ; with other holidays, and being allowed to fee their friends, which of courfe means their " young man." Being, thank heaven, once more in fmooth waters, with excellent fervants, which I am happy to find ftill *can* be had, clean, competent, obedient, truftworthy, and attached, I can laugh, though not without a retrofpective fhudder, at the bitter trials I have had in this way. One gigantic drum-major in petticoats that I had, was of fuch a diabolical temper, with fuch a vulgar Billingfgate way of fhowing it, that fhe frightened not only me but the whole houfe, and did not even know how to fweep a carpet properly ; and as I had for many years a firft-rate houfemaid, who was in fact a perfect furniture doctor, and had fecrets for keeping oil-paintings, carvings, bronzes, mirrors, and all forts of *bric-à-brac* in perfection, I told the drum-major all thefe, and infifted upon having all my things kept up as they had always been; at firft fhe refifted, doing fo in the moft infolent manner; at laft, when fhe found how my ways of doing things fimplified her work, and abridged the time it took, fhe condefcended to fay one day, " Yes," or as fhe pronounced it, "*Yaas*, I don't fay but what your way is the beft, for I fee it is now." "That," faid I, "is not the point; beft or worft, I choofe to have things done in my own way in my own houfe." Added to her infolence, fhe was very ungrateful and equally difhoneft, and fo offenfively rude to every one, that I threatened to report her conduct to the lady who had recommended her to me as a treafure of honefty, and good temper!

" *She* did not care for Mrs. ——, nor for me, nor for any one; and *fhe* was not going down upon her knees to people with that cringing civility that the other fervants did!"

" Ah," faid I, " you had better kneel to God, and pray to Him to change your heart and temper."

" God's nothing to me!" was her horrible anfwer.

" I fear not," I replied.

While another *lady* of the fame genus, upon my daring to tell her that fhe fhould not have let one of the bed-room fires go out, clenched her fift and ftamped her foot as fhe vociferated, " Ah! the gentry will foon get no fervants at all, and be obliged to do their own work,—that's what we are trying for!"

" We have to do our own work now," faid I, "and to pay fervants very dearly at the fame time for not doing it; but don't you think, for your *own* fakes, fo long as you condefcend to take our money and eat our bread, it would be better, and more to your own advantage, if you conducted yourfelves a little more confcientioufly?   I am not for one moment faying that you are not quite as good, or even a great deal better, than we are; but *that* has nothing to do with it. Suppofe the pofitions were reverfed, and I was obliged to become your fervant to-morrow; there would be no earthly ufe in thinking what I was born to, or what I had been accuftomed to; you would then be my miftrefs; and though all my ways would be very different from yours, it would not only be my duty but my intereft, in return for the food and wages you gave me, to endeavour to pleafe and conform to your requirements in every way that I could, inftead of raifing a ftandard of rebellion at every order you gave me."

Well, this amiable democrat ended by going upon the ftreets, and the drum-major got a place with a falfe character, which at all events muft have been better than her real one.

Another young lady—alfo, of the genus houfemaid—living in a clergyman's family, having let her mafter out, was about to refaften the hall door, when his little boy, who was in the hall, faid, "You need not do that, Jane, for your mafter will be back directly."

"Who do you mean by *my mafter?*" cried the Amazon, turning fiercely round and glaring at the child.

" Why, papa, to be fure."

" He 's not *my* mafter, he 's my employer ! "

While a young lady at a National fchool in the country, who was wafting her time over a little bit of ufelefs crochet, which fhe had converted into a fort of cotton blackamoor, which never could be fcrubbed white, while her ftockings were well ventilated with large holes; upon my faying to her—

" Now Mary, inftead of wafting your time upon that perfectly ufelefs crochet, don't you think it would be better if you mended your ftockings?"

" Pleafe um, mother don't like me to mend ftockings; fhe fays as it ain't *gen*-teel."

All this infubordination and ftuckupativenefs combined it is, which is the moral dry-rot that is fapping the foundations of fociety. What all England requires to be taught, the higher quite as much as the lower orders, is, that WORK is about the moft ennobling thing in the world; and as *every* fort of work *muft* and ought to be done,—there is in reality no fuch thing as "menial work"—that bogean myth, which middle-clafs vulgarity fo dreads. The only really menial, and therefore degrading things, are, idlenefs, ufeleffnefs, dependence, fhams, fubftitutes, braggadocia, and worldlinefs; which latter, is the nucleus of all vulgarity—VULGARMINDEDNESS.

HAPPY JACK.

HERE can be no doubt that the flat-
nefs, ftalenefs, unprofitablenefs, and
inanity of Englifh life arife from its
block machinery fort of uniformity,
and total want of individuality in thought, action,
or character; its echo and follow-my-leader fort
of conventionality, which caufes anything like
originality or independence of opinion or action,
in the rafh perpetrator of either, to pafs for
mad or bad; and be tabooed accordingly. Unlefs
indeed the faid individual happens to be exceptionally rich, as every thing is "*for the million*" now-a-days, whether financially or focially
fpeaking, or elfe placed on the pinnacle of
the world's flippery high places; *then* indeed,
eccentricities, however outrageous, or vices,
however flagrant and notorious, not only pafs
unchallenged, but are cited with laudation, as
proofs of genius and fuperiority, and ferve to

form additional hecatombs of truth and juſtice to
the foul national fetiſh, PUBLIC LIFE! which, ſo
far as politicians go, might be deſcribed in the
identical words of the keeper of a menagerie,
who addreſſed a ſchool of young gentlemen as
follows:—

" This ere hanimal, my little dears, is a leopard.
His complexion is yaller, and agreeably diwerſi-
fied with black ſpots. It vos a wulgar herror
of the hancients, that the critter vos hincapable
of changin his ſpots; vich vos diſproved in
modern times, by obſerwin that he wery fre-
quently ſlept in one ſpot, and next night changed
to another, cordin as it ſuited him beſt."

And there is ſomething ſo exceptionally petri-
fying in the whole arcana of political life, that
the American epitaph upon the miſer who died
of ſoftening of the brain, would do admirably
for that of moſt " diſtinguiſhed members of the
legiſlature," viz.:—

" His head gave way, but his hand never did.
His brain ſoftened, but his heart never could."
But leaving all this block machinery, let us go
into the highways and byways, and ſee if we
cannot pick up ſomething like character, freſh-
neſs, and originality, among the weeds and wild
flowers, that are hedged within their little ſpheres
by the roadſide. It ſo happened, that in walking
the other day to Foreſt-hill I was caught in one

of thofe drenching fhowers, that have been fo prevalent during this fevere fummer of 1876. But fortunately there came rattling by, a return cab, which I ftopped, and got in. The man drove me to my deftination, at Foreft-hill, where I remained about half-an-hour, the cabman having, to my great fatisfaction, driven his horfe and himfelf, under the fhelter of a hofpitable archway. On my return, long before I reached my own gate, the fky became blue and cloudlefs, and

> " No fun upon an Eafter day
> Is half fo fine a fight "

as that fun was, playing bopeep with the hawthorns and acacias and among the white horfe-cheftnuts and the glorious rich red Spanifh cheftnut bloffoms. So that, being particularly ftruck by the gloffy coat, and, for a hack, the unufually fat fleek fides of the bright bay, full-fized, high-ftepping cab-horfe, I ftopped to pat him and give him fome green boughs, as he was trying to gather a falad for himfelf; then, turning to the cabman, I complimented him upon the high condition of his horfe, which, as I told him, was much to his credit, as it fhowed what good care he took of him.

" Ay; care in courfe I takes on him," faid he, twirling a ftraw in his mouth. "But care be blowed! It ain't *that* as does it; it 's his mind."

Thinking a horſe "with a mind" ought to have a name, I aſked, "What do you call him? what is his name?"

"Well, his *criſſen* name is Jack, but I calls him 'Happy Jack,' for 'tis his mind as does it; for he's *that* contented and happy in his mind, that if he war fed upon tenpenny nails and pack-thread, he'd be in better condition than any ofs in England. Yer ſee he don't never let nothink put him out, don't Jack; he juſt takes the world as it goes."·

"As moſt cab-horſes do," I put in.

"Ay, but that don't pervent Jack having pinions of his own; but he keeps 'em to his ſelf, and takes the world as it goes."

"In ſhort, he don't, let his *pinions* fly away with him?"

"That's about it. Jack knows what's what, but when he comes in *contac* with them as knows nothing, he never interferes with their little ſtock in trade."

"Truly a wiſe horſe, a moſt wiſe horſe; and like all wiſe heads, he has a ſilent tongue in his."

"Then yer ſee, 'tain't only his mind, but he can eat hany think "——

"That he has a mind to?" I put in.

"No, hany think; gloves, boots, horange peel, money—hany think "—ſpreading the two florin pieces I had juſt given him on the palm

of his hand, and offering them to the omni-
vorous Jack of the great mind, and corre-
fponding appetite.

"Ah," faid I, "nothing eafier than to eat
money ; but, poor fellow, let him eat his, in oats,
and don't make him fwallow thofe."

"Why not ? I allus tells him as he's the beft
right to the money, as he arns it ; but carrots is
his turtle and wenfon, only there ain't none worth
eating now but French ones, and they's dear."

"Well, tell me where Jack's ftable is, and I'll
fend him a hamper of French carrots."

"Ho ! will yer though ? well, I'm uncommon
obleeged to yer ! That's fuft rate !"

"I will indeed, for I think very well of you,
for being fo fond of your horfe."

"Fond on him ! I fhould think fo. The parfon
fays it's wicked, when I fays my miffus and the
kids is all very well in their places, but that place
is not afore Jack ; for in pint of clevernefs they
are not fit to hold a pail of water to him. Then
yer fee, this is the way on it : I fticks up all the
more and thinks a deal the more on him, hon
account of hall the lies, hill natur, and defamation
he's fubjec to hon account of my mates being
henvious of him and me ; they never have a
good word to fay of either on us ; they tells my
fares that I fhall upfet the cab, that Jack's a
roarer, and that he jibs !"

"Well, they fibs," faid I.

"And no miftake! Did yer ever fee water through a folar *mikerfcope*, marm?—with all them devils let loofe, a devouring, a running down, and a tearing on heach other to pieces? Vell, *that's* the world to a hair; fo no wonder fo many poor critters wifhes, and takes theirfelves out of it."

In my own mind, I fo perfectly endorfed the truth of the cabman's fimile, that I thought it better to end this philofophical *féance* with a Burleighan nod of the head to him, and another pat of the fat fides of that "paragon of animals," Jack. But there was fuch quinteffential truth, in what this poor man had faid of his compeers' ufage of his excellent and therefore much calumniated equine friend, that it fet me thinking that the world's opinion of moft perfons, is as various as that of hiftorians and biographers, on that of Edward Lord Clarendon, who was alternately deified and defamed for party purpofes. Southey declares him to have been the wifeft and moft upright of ftatefmen, while Brodie does not hefitate to reprefent him as a miferable fycophant and canting hypocrite; and Hume, on the other hand, embalms him with the greateft refpect and admiration. Hallam is cautious and timid in his praife,—that worft, becaufe leaft honeft, fpecies of condemnation. Agar Ellis unhefitatingly pronounces him an unprincipled man of talent. The old ftory of the chameleon, might greatly aid a correct folution of thefe divers contradictory opinions, both as regards public and private characters; and thus award to each feparate and oppofing verdict its quota of truth. But in the midft of much that is dubious in all fuch matters, one thing at leaft is certain, and that is, that none of thefe judgments individually, no, nor taken all collectively, can ever hit upon the true inter-dependencies and fequences of events, at all accurately; any more than they can upon their origin. And how fhould they? Since the *real* motives of our actions are for the moft part fo fubtile and concrete, as to become, even to ourfelves, a " great firft caufe, leaft underftood." But all thefe are only pfychological experiments *in corpore vili*, alias human nature; fo, to return to the nobler, becaufe the more innocent animal, the poor cab-horfe,—the next morning, his devoted flave, alias his mafter, came for his hamper of carrots. " Happy Jack " indeed! to whom happinefs was fo eafy! Unlike the world's little great men, to whom hampers of kingdoms, make happinefs impoffible.

MACAULAY.

 WISH I had the honour of know-
ing Mr. Trevelyan perſonally, that I
might have the pleaſure of thanking
him *vivâ voce* for the immenſe boon
he has beſtowed upon *me individually*, irreſpec-
tive of my being one of the atoms that make up
the world at large, by his publication of "The
Life and Letters" of his exceptionally gifted and
diſtinguiſhed kinſman, the really great Thomas
Babington Macaulay. It is given to ſo few of us
here below, to complete the cycle of our thought,
and ſtill leſs, to realize that of our *ideal,* that
what greater boon can one human being beſtow
upon another, than the proofs that one at leaſt
of his or her golden idols had *not* feet of clay,
and that, though albeit of coloſſal dimenſions, the
ore was pure and unalloyed from ſummit to baſe ?
And this is preciſely the incalculable ſervice which

Mr. Trevelyan[1] has juſt rendered me.   I never was, even in my " ſalad days," much addicted to hero-worſhip ; I believe thoſe who live much among what are called " celebrities " ſeldom are, they being too nearly in the ſame category as ſupers and ſcene-ſhifters in a theatre, who ſee too much of the ugly machinery, paint, and tinſel, to be capable of winding themſelves up to admiration point at the fineſt and moſt glittering transformation ſcene ever produced ; however marvellous the effect may be upon thoſe outſiders, called " the public," who know or ſee nothing of the *modus operandi ;* but—

> " In that ſoft amber light of long ago."

From the very firſt appearance of " Knight's Quarterly Magazine," wherein I made Macaulay's acquaintance—alas ! only in print—the cultus I then and there offered up at the altar of his genius, has gone on ſteadily increaſing in devotion, as in the courſe of time diſcrimination has been grafted upon enthuſiaſm.   It was on " A Night in Ancient Rome," that I firſt meet him,—that gem *par excellence*, from the antique, ſo wondrouſly and clearly inciſed to the moſt delicately minute touches, ſo exquiſitely and highly poliſhed, not only externally but inter-

---

[1] M.P. for the Border Boroughs.

nally, that even he himfelf, though ever working up to the fame pinnacle, never furpaffed it. Poor Praed, too, fo charming as far as he went, the "Vivian Joyeufe" of "Knight's Quarterly," confirmed me in my new creed, and told me I did not and could not overrate Macaulay, and promifed that fome day he would make him known to me. Woe is me! that "fome day," like fo many other "fome days," never came. Had he lived perhaps it might. Well! who knows, but in the "good time coming," which never comes on this fide Styx, all our days may be thefe happy long due "fome days?" Of courfe it did not need Mr. Trevelyan's upon the whole very able life of his illuftrious uncle, to additionally fpread the fame of Macaulay's *genius* from pole to pole, but it *did* need it to fet the feal of genuinenefs upon the MAN—the hall-mark upon his virtues—which, though outlined very plainly, even through the dazzling effulgence of his great intellectual folar light, could not, of courfe, be verified in detail. It was impoffible to read a fentence Macaulay ever wrote or fpoke, even in that great arena of humbug, and fham Areopagus, St. Stephen's, without *feeling* that all *was* what it profeffed to be. Even his wondrous and unapproachable ftyle, was as natural and fpontaneous, as the rufhing water-worlds of Niagara, or the rich gorgeous fertility of tropical vegetation. You *felt* by intuition that he did not, as it is called, " get up" the fubject ; but that it was all the infallible refult of the richnefs of the indigenous foil, evenly, carefully, and fcientifically handled and cultivated, then fown with endlefs variety of the choiceft and beft kinds of feed, which only required the genial auxiliaries of time, feafon, and atmofpheric influences, to produce their inevitably luxuriant crops; where it was fo manifeft that to the planting of Paul and the watering of Apollos, God had fo glorioufly and unlimitedly given the increafe.

Yes, in all he wrote, in all he faid, in all he did, you felt that the greatnefs, that is, the goodnefs, of the man was genuine ; *he* could not *act* a part, becaufe the one, nature had intended him to create in the world's drama was too noble a one. Like all fingle-minded, broad, deep, natures, he had the courage of, not only his opinions, but of his likes or diflikes, in great things or fmall, with the ftream for, or againft it. This it was, which caufed him never to lofe an opportunity of denouncing and detecting, that arch-charlatan and vulgar-minded felf-feeker and felf-worfhipper, Henry, Lord Brougham; or of proclaiming amid any amount of fneers, ironical fmiles, and raifed eyebrows, his love and admiration of " Clariffa Harlowe." Of courfe it was only poor, patient, perfecuted Clariffa that he loved, and of courfe he had an equally ftrong and laudable wifh to have ftrangled the whole of the Harlowe family, and have fold Harlowe Place after, for a private madhoufe ; and regretted that there was a chronological impoffibility exifting to prevent his having had the fatisfaction of even fo tardily having rid the world, of that typical fine gentleman, Mr. Lovelace. Nay, more, I have not the leaft doubt that he not only would have endorfed but even had admired ! defpite the " Lays of Ancient Rome," that fonnet " To the Author of Clariffa," which appeared in the fecond edition of Richardfon's beft work :—

" To the Author of Clarissa.

" O mafter of the heart ! whofe magick fkill
　The clofe receffes of the foul can find ;
　Can roufe, becalm, and terrify the mind,
Now melt with pity, now with anguifh thrill.

Thy moral page, while virtuous precepts fill,
　Warm from the heart, to mend the age defigned,
　Wit, ftrength, truth, decency, are all combin'd,
To lead our youth to good and guard from ill.

O long enjoy what thou fo well haft won,—
　The grateful tribute of each honeft heart,
Sincere, nor hackney'd in the ways of men ;
At each diftrefsful ftroke their true tears run,
　And nature, unfophifticate by art,
Owns and applauds the labours of thy pen."

But if Macaulay had never uttered or written a ſyllable but the golden axioms contained in the following excerpt from Mr. Trevelyan's juſt-publiſhed " Life " of him, they alone, would have ſufficed to immortalize him, as a practical outcome of his true and honeſt nature, illuſtrated by his own choice :—

" I often wonder what ſtrange infatuation leads men who can do ſomething better, to ſquander their intellect, their health, their energy on such objects as thoſe which moſt ſtateſmen are engaged in purſuing. . . . . That a man before whom the two paths, of literature and politics, lie open, and who might hope for eminence in either, ſhould chooſe politics and quit literature, ſeems to me madneſs.   On the one ſide is health, leiſure, peace of mind, the ſearch after truth, and all the enjoyments of friendſhip and converſation : on the other ſide, is almoſt certain ruin to the conſtitution, conſtant labour, conſtant anxiety. Every friendſhip which a man may have, becomes precarious, as ſoon as he engages in politics. . . . . Who would compare the fame of Charles Townſhend, to that of Hume ? that of Lord North to that of Gibbon ? that of Lord Chatham to that of Johnſon ?"

Yes; but the moſt extraordinary infatuation of all is, that as the great ambition of this ſort of men is *to live*, that is, to go down to poſterity, they cannot comprehend that nothing *can* live but what has life in it, and there is no vitality in anything but the *real*, and alike for the moſt exalted, as well as for the meaneſt intellect, their daily and hourly chequered life, of hopes, fears, duties, trials, ſtruggles, ſorrows, affections, diſlikes, temptations, the warring againſt them, or ſuccumbing to them; in a word, each human being's ſchool of ſelf-diſcipline is his *only real* and immortal life, and not the adventitious external circumſtances by which he is ſurrounded, whether they be the pomps and vanities or the perils and pauperiſm of earth's lottery. But the fact is, that worldlineſs is the moſt vulgar-minded and vulgariſing, as it is nearly the moſt univerſal of all vices; and like Death it enters everywhere, for it is quite as often found on the higheſt rung of the ladder, among thoſe born in the purple, as in the ſuburban villa or behind a counter. A mind like Macaulay's would naturally recoil from the ſewers and ceſſpools of political life, but he was only one of the few exceptions that prove the rule, for there can be no doubt that PUBLIC LIFE is the great *fetiſh* of England, and the wholeſale ſacrifices made to it, and for it, are even more unſpeakably and revoltingly hideous than thoſe of its African prototypes. And what wonder? when it is no matter how worthleſs, unprincipled, and immoral a man's private or real life may be, *that*, is completely ignored, and never for a moment makes him ineligible for not only afpiring to but obtaining the higheft pofitions in public life, which only require a certain amount and verfatility of brain power and unlimited moral elafticity. For half-a-dozen Macaulays in the world, who can comprehend and feel that though, of courfe, nepotifm and back-ftair influence can and do beftow power and pofition, there are no fuch things as real honours except thofe which have been honourably earned or nobly won. Yet I am fure there is hardly a fecond, who would have had the honeft fimplicity to have evinced his gladnefs as he did, when his unfought peerage was offered him. Still, it was quite in keeping with the whole tenour of his life, which was, to confer benefits upon all who came within his reach; and verily, if any honour there were in this cafe, it was moft unqueftionably all on the fide of the peerage.

But public men, in their infatiable cravings for what they imagine to be immortality [?] forget what ironical jades the Fates are, and how TIME, who ought to be old enough to refpect what fo efpecially belongs to him, aids and abets them in their iconoclaftic pranks. The prefent and the future have their intereft, at their refpective antipodes. For inftance, if in thefe days of railways and electric telegraphs, any one got a letter putting him confidentially *au fait* of the projected "Royal Titles Bill," five days, or even four-and-twenty hours, before the newſpapers were on the ſcent of it, even if it did not afford any great delight, or indignation, or intereſt, to the recipient of the letter, it would do ſo as goſſip capital for the viſitors and neighbours of the favoured receiver of the early intelligence. Yet juſt put the dial on two or three hundred years, and no one then living will care one ſtraw about the "Royal Titles Bill," from the child that learns all about it hiſtorically as a taſk in the ſchool-room, to the child's parent, who liſtens to it as a duty from the child at ſecond hand. But if, indeed, ſome private letters of this time ſhould turn up, were they only from Queen Victoria's real *femme de chambre* (not miſtreſs of the robes) to a ſiſter Abigail in London, ſtating that—

" Has her Majeſty is to be made a Hempreſs, which I don't conſider no ſuch great matter for a Hengliſh queen, taint as hif ſhe was one of them furreners, nor hif indeed as they was a going to raiſe her ſalary with it, that would be a different thing; but all I looks to his, that praps it will hadd to *my* dooties conſiderable, has of courſe the eads will be wore higher than hever, and I not a penny the better for it; but hif there hain't that 'ere dreſſing-room bell on the rampage again. I'll write from Gummany next week. So no more at prefent, from

" Yours truly,
" Dorothy Dresser "

—this charming epiftle would excite more intereft and converfation from one end of the kingdom to the other, than the moft ftirring political events of the prefent day will in pofterity of three hundred years' growth. We enjoy, it is true, fo far as a laugh goes, that piece of ftale politics called " Queen Elizabeth's golden fpeech," *i.e.*, her laft to her Parliament, wherein fhe told them that all the glories and improvements during her reign, were due wholly and folely to her own wifdom and prefcience, but all the fhort-comings and mifcarriages "*were their culps ;*" yet ftill *we* fhould now take much more intereft in hearing how many "Sirrahs" fhe beftowed upon her grooms for "*their culps,*" when fhe remounted her palfrey on her return to her palace, or how many "fwinging" boxes on the ear fhe beftowed upon her mifchievous maids of honour, when fhe difcovered that they had rouged the tip of her nofe inftead of her cheeks. And who, now-a-days, cares one jot for the political and public affairs in " The Pafton Letters"? One is glad, indeed, that Judge Yelverton's fpiteful pamphlet, trving to make out the Paftons were

villains, or *glebæ afcripti*, was eventually dif-
proved; and alfo, that though the Duke of
Northumberland did efcheat, or *tout bonnement*
cheat, poor John Pafton out of Caifter Caftle,
which bluff Sir John Faftolf had left him, it was
afterwards reftored to the family. But how
much more intereft does one take even in the
"worfted doublet which his wife Margaret
brought John Pafton from Worfted, when fhe
went to fee him in London;" and of which he
found the threads "almoft like filk." And moft
interefting are the parental outburfts of affection
in the fhape of "good thrafhings," regularly
twice a week, of Elizabeth Pafton, or the "head
broken in two or three places," from the fame
weekly allowance to her Aunt Margery. One
only regrets that there is not a graphic defcription of the *mife en fcène*, *i.e.*, the furniture and
dimenfions of the room in which this more than
monaftic difcipline took place; and likewife, as
they were fuch notable houfewives and "fkilful
leeches" in thofe days, that after their precious
balms had broken their children's heads, they do
not tell us what precious ointments they applied
to heal them. Their exact and refpective dreffes
and coifs, too, are great omiffions, as well as
the not clearly fpecifying with what implements
the caftigations were adminiftered,—birch, cane,
flipper, or cat? As for poor Margery Pafton,

"who fadly demeaned herfelf" by marrying
Richard Calle, a faithful dependent of the Paftons, and was turned out of the houfe for per-
fifting in her intention, by John the Second, who
faid that "Calle fhould never have his good
will to make his fifter fell candles and muftard
at Framlingham,"—I wifh I had been there to
have helped her in my little way, by giving an
order, not indeed that the gas fhould have been
cut off in the lower regions, feeing that in thofe
days they had none, but that nothing but tallow
fhould be burned in the Netherlands, that every
thing fhould be dreffed *à la tartare*, and that all
the maids (for of courfe the men would not
have fubmitted—they never do—to anything;
which proves their fuperiority,) well, yes, that
all the maids fhould have worn muftard plafters
en permanence, whether they had colds or not—
which, living in Norfolk, of courfe they would
have had, or ought to have had, all the year
round.

As for the abfence of all family affection
among us Englifh, that feemed to fo puzzle and
aftound all foreigners in thofe days, and caufed
the Venetian Ambaffador to doubt whether in
high or low life any Englifhman ever could have
been in love; I am fure we modern Englifh
have no changes or innovations in domefticities
to reproach ourfelves with. Any little maudlin

family affection we may be encumbered with, there is always self-intereft, like the Queen's Proctor in the Divorce Court, "intervening" to adjuft the balance; fo that

> " Love light as air, at fight of human ties,
> Plumes his light wings, and in a moment flies."

But, as we are alfo told that whatever abfence of affection there might be in the Englifh of the fourteenth, fifteenth, and fixteenth centuries, they were remarkable for their good breeding and extreme politenefs, this proves to us what a total lofs we *urfa majors* of the nineteenth century have fuftained. If there was any chance of infufing a little, even a few drops of this loft life-blood into them, one would almoft be tempted to recommend a courfe of educational vivifection, after the manner of the Paftonian weekly thrafh-ings and broken heads, for the rifing generation.

But as a more modern and illuftrious inftance of the vitality of reality reaching to immortality, in fact, the only well authenticated proof of the truth of the Darwinian theory of " the furvival of the fitteft," Macaulay's family muft, as a matter of courfe, be juftly proud of his genius and his fame, a pride that will defcend to his lateft pofterity; but for the immediate portion of it ftill living, I feel fure that, great and immortal as that genius and fame are, they are yet the two attributes which, when recalling him, the family dwell on leaſt. No, it is the kind, conſiderate, ever ſympathetic and affectionate friend, the large-hearted, genial, many-ſided good man, who not only thought of giving dinner parties to children in his rooms at the Albany, for that would have been nothing, but who invariably had the thought and took the trouble of ſeeing that everything was got that his little gueſts could poſſibly like. Ah! great univerſal mother NATURE, there *you*, as always, ſat enſhrined and paramount in the heart, the deep, pure heart, of this great man, though his intellect *was* brilliant-cut, and flaſhed its myriad facets upon liſtening ſenates, and an admiring world. No wonder, not that his family, which was *his* nucleus, but that all who came within the ſphere of his influence, loved him; not, by all accounts, from any perſonal graces or charm of manner, for it was ſaid that in appearance he was ungainly; no, it was the ſheer triumph of mind, ay, and of ſoul, over matter; crowned by that impalpable but ſubtle and divine halo which goodneſs ſheds around all who poſſeſs it.

I would have given more than I poſſeſs or am ever likely to poſſeſs, to have been an inviſible eye and ear witneſs to the ſcene of *his* "arreſt of the five members"—I mean when the five irate Quakers waited upon him at the Albany, to

expoſtulate with him about the too life-like portrait he had limned of their idol William Penn.
" Its tone," as Mr. Trevelyan truly ſays, " reminds
one of Johnſon," only from its conciliating effect
it muſt have lacked the other leviathan's ſledge-
hammerativeneſs."

" I wrote," ſaid Macaulay, in reply to their
complaint, " the hiſtory of four years, during
which he was expoſed to great temptations;
during which he was the favourite of a bad king
and an active ſolicitor in a moſt corrupt court.
His character was injured by the aſſociations.
Ten years before, or ten years later, he would
have made a much better figure. But was I to
begin my book ten years ſooner or later for
William Penn's ſake ? "

" His viſitors," adds Mr. Trevelyan, " complimented him upon his courteſy and candour,
and parted from him on the beſt of terms."

So I ſhould ſuppoſe; but though Cæſar (Julius),
as Suetonius tells us, lacked the *vis comica*, and
therefore with all his greatneſs muſt have been
but a dull fellow, Macaulay did not, ſo it is *his*
face that I ſhould ſo much like to have ſeen,
after the departure of the five Quakers. If they
had only been " Friends in Council" and knew
how to keep their own, they might have known
before they came, that *their* Penn could have had
no poſſible chance againſt Macaulay's.

I am now glad that I did not ſee his face, for it would have been that ſupererogatory thing, an additional ſorrow, to be among thoſe who

> "Ne'er can look upon that face again."

Truly,

> " His body is buried in peace,
> But his name liveth for evermore."

PROPOSED PLAN FOR A SUPPLE-MENTARY COLLEGE TO THE UNIVERSITIES,

FOR THE PURPOSE OF SAVING TIME AND TROUBLE WITH RESPECT TO UNDERGRADUATES LIKELY TO BE PLUCKED.

FOLLOWED BY TWO GHOST STORIES.

"THERE is a river," faith my friend Burton (not Burton-upon-Trent) " at the Swallow, that finketh into the earth and rifeth again two miles nearer Leatherhead. They do fay a goofe was put in, and came out again alive, though with the lofs of all its feathers."

This would appear to be a far fhorter and more fwimming mode of plucking than the ordinary procefs in ufe at the Univerfities, fo we ftrongly recommend that the propofed Supplementary Plucking College fhould be built at the *Swallow;* and the vicinity to Leatherhead is another congenial defideratum that would make the *pluckee* feel quite *en pays de connaiſſance* at the little light dinner, given by Godfrey Nevil, brother to the great Earl of Warwick, in 1470, at his palace at York, to a few of his friends among the nobles, clergy, and gentry, wherein he ſpent 300 quarters of wheat, 330 tuns of ale, 104 tuns of wine, one pipe of ſpiced wine, 80 fat oxen, ſix wild bulls[!], 1,004 ſheep, 300 hogs, 3,000 calves, 3,000 geeſe, 2,000 capons, 300 pigs, 100 peacocks, 200 cranes, 200 kids, 2,000 chickens, 4,000 pigeons, 4,000 rabbits, 240 bitterns, 4,000 ducks, 400 herons, 200 pheaſants, 500 partridges, 4,000 woodcocks, 400 plovers, 100 curlews, 100 quails, 1,000 egrets, 200 rees, above 400 bucks, does, and roebucks, 1,056 hot veniſon paſties, 4,000 cold veniſon paſties, 1,000 diſhes of jelly parted, 4,000 diſhes of jelly plain, 4,000 cold porpoiſes [!] and 400 tarts, 4,000 cold cuſtards, 2,000 hot, 300 breams, 8 ſeales.

At this feaſt the Earl of Warwick was ſteward, the Earl of Bedford treaſurer, the Lord Haſtings comptroller, with many other noble officers. And there were 1,000 ſervitors, 62 cooks, 515 ſcullions, and innumerable turnſpit dogs. It is ſad to add that in a few years after giving theſe agreeable little dinners (as will ſometimes happen in more modern times), this poor gentleman fell into difficulties and died in great diſtreſs, or as the chronicle fets forth, " The king feized on his eftate and fent him prifoner into France, where he was bound in chains[1] and died in great poverty. Juftice," concludes this Jofeph Hume of an hiftorian, "thus punifhing his former prodigality."

But dear me ! if we are to believe all, ay, or even *half* we hear, the above little *ambigu* was nothing to the way in which thofe ecclefiaftical commons, the monks, ate, and thofe *too well* protected females, the nuns, drank. Juft liften to the requirements of a king's daughter and a king's fifter in that way, according to Rymer. As there was no *Times* newfpaper in thofe days with philanthropic advertifers, anxious " to receive as inmates, Ladies [!], and Gentlemen of intemperate habits," we muft charitably hope that in this inftance it was not *in vino veritas*.

But here is the little item :

" In 1307," fays Rymer, " Edward the Second confirmed the grant his father, Edward the Firft, had made to his fifter, Mary, a Nun at AMBROSEBURY, of 200*l. per annum*, 40 oak trees for firing in her chamber,[2] and 20 *dolia*

---

[1] Like Lord Bateman, without, however, meeting with a " Fair Sophia," which would not have been proper for an archbifhop, and altogether inconvenient in the event of his being recalled from exile, as there were no coaches and three in thofe days to bring her back in, and the Church was his legitimate bride.

[2] Surely it muft have been too hot to hold her !

[or hogſheads] of wine, as long as ſhe continued in the Nunnery and lived in England.[1] And," adds the innocent Rymer, " the reader will not, I believe, be diſpleaſed to ſee the care that was taken in thoſe days for the *ſuſtentation* of the daughter and ſiſter of a king of England." Whereupon he gives the following ſtate paper : " The *King* to the *Sheriff* of *Wilts*, greeting.

" Foraſmuch as we are indebted to our deareſt ſiſter *Mary*, a *Nun of Ambroſebury*, in the ſumm of 12*l*. 7*s*. 3*d*. As well for hay, oats, litter, and ſhooing, as for her ſervants wages, whileſt ſhe tarried at *Windſor*, in the month of *December* laſt paſt, as alſo for her expenſes in travelling from *Windſor* to *Ambroſebury*, as in a Bill of our *Warderobe*, delivered by our ſiſter into our Chancery, appears more at large. We, willing to ſatisfy our ſiſter in the particular with all ſpeed we may, do hereby command you to pay to our ſaid ſiſter, or her lawful *Attorney*, the ſaid ſumme out of the iſſues of your Bailifry, without Delay ; and we in our accounts at your Exchequer ſhall make all due allowance for the ſame.

" *Witneſſe the King at* Windſor, Jan. the 1ſt, 1313.

    " By a *Bill of the* Warderobe."

---

[1] She muſt, in a meaſure, have infringed the contract by being often half-ſeas over.

But though I cannot, friend Reader, feaſt you with a thouſand hecatombs like Godfrey Nevil, nor fluſh you with twenty dolias of wine, like the royal Nun of Ambroſebury, yet I can, in order to " ſpeed the parting gueſt," act upon a ſage axiom of another old chronicler, Ingulfus, who opined that " However dull a *Boke* might be at ye onſet, and even in ye maine parts thereofe ; it ſhould not faile to have a *ſpirate* in ye ende."

Therefore I ſhall conclude with *two* ſpirits, by giving you a brace of well authenticated ghoſt ſtories, as told to me ſome years ago by the two ſtill living actors in them, a lady and a gentleman, both of a certain age and pre-eminently *un*imaginative, or what is vulgarly called *not* given to romancing. One happened in broad daylight to an enthuſiaſtic diſciple of Iſaac Walton, while angling the ſultry ſummer hours away. This I ſhould have conſidered unique, and therefore apocryphal, in the archives of ghoſtology, except for the many ghoſts who began to ſee daylight about the reign of George I. according to Andrew Moreton, in that curious collection of ſupernatural biographies of his, entitled " THE SECRETS OF THE INVISIBLE WORLD DISCLOSED, OR AN UNIVERSAL HISTORY OF APPARITIONS, SACRED AND PROFANE, UNDER ALL DENOMINATIONS, *whether* ANGELICAL, DIABOLICAL, OR HUMAN SOULS DEPARTED; with a great variety of furprifing and diverting examples never publifhed before; alfo fhowing how we may diftinguifh between the APPARITIONS OF GOOD AND EVIL SPIRITS, and how we ought to behave to them.

> "'SPIRITS, in whatfoever fhape they chufe,
> Dilated or condens'd, bright or obfcure,
> Can execute their airy purpofes,
> And works of love or enmity fulfil.'—MILTON.

Sold by Thomas Worral, at Judge Coke's Head, againft St. Dunftan's Church, Fleet Streeet. MDCCXXXV."

The copper plates are not the leaft curious part of this book, next to the open and ftraightforward proceedings of the apparitions; moft of which travel by fields, lanes, and gardens, knock at cedar-parlour windows at noon-day, are feen of more than one perfon, and, moft marvellous of all, for the moft part belong to *living* bodies, who in order not to bear the brunt of their fantaftic doings, go to great trouble and expenfe to prove an *alibi* of feveral miles', and often feveral hundreds of miles', diftance, at the time their fpirits were fo unwarrantably pawning their honour and getting duplicates of their forms. But there is not ONE in the Moreton collection, in my opinion, half fo wonderful as the two well authenticated, not to fay "well-conditioned" apparitions, I fhall now have the honour of prefenting to you.

" There are more things in heaven and earth, Horatio,
Than are dreamt of in your philoſophy."—HAMLET.

Place aux dames! even though we are going
ſo much out of the world.   It is now ſome five-
and-twenty years ſince I became acquainted, in a
German town, with two ſiſters, of the claſs I de-
nominate "ſenſible women," vulgarly called "old
maids."   They were not only ſenſible, but, like
moſt really ſenſible people, extremely agreeable
and well-informed, the eldeſt particularly ſo, who
had for many years rubbed up againſt Göthe
and Jean Paul, while ſhe occupied a poſt in the
little court of Weimar.   But if *ſhe* had it in the
head her ſiſter carried off the palm in heart, for a
more thoroughly lovable, amiable, unſelfiſh perſon
it would not be eaſy to find ; but then, to be ſure,
ſhe had graduated in that moſt humanizing and
mellowing of all ſchools—affliction, and drawn
her ſympathy for others, from the deep ſource of
a great perſonal ſorrow ; not that there was any
ſurface ſadneſs or even penſiveneſs about her ;
on the contrary, her manner was *enjouée* and
prévenante, always ready to promote or join in
any of thoſe thouſand little *jeux de ſociété* which
paſs away an evening ſo pleaſantly, and which
French woman (for they were French, not
German,) ſo pre-eminently poſſeſs the ſecret of
making graceful as well as amuſing.   Still, at

times, deſpite her cheerful manner, a deep ſhadow would ſteal over her perfectly pale face, giving it that intenſely deſolate and unearthly look which a ſnow landſcape aſſumes when a gorgeous ſun ſuddenly ſets, taking with it all the red and golden roſes it had but the minute before been ſtrewing on that wintry winding-ſheet. She always dreſſed in black, but merely rich black ſilk, not mourning properly ſo called. Nevertheleſs, ſhe had acquired the *ſobriquet* of " the widow," and the miſſes (for there *are* miſſes, even in Germany, as well as ſentimental ſauſage-eating *Fräuleins*), yea, verily, even the miſſes giggled when they ſpoke of her as ſuch, and my curioſity being piqued to know how ſhe had acquired this honorary freedom of the conjugal ſtate, upon inquiry I was told that thereby hung, not only a romantic tale, but a ghoſt ſtory,—that Mademoiſelle Stéphanie de A—— had, fifteen years previouſly to the time of which I am writing, been engaged to be married to a M. Vander—ſomething—a Dutchman. Everything was arranged, the day fixed, and they were to be married in a month, when he was accidentally drowned. To this part of the cataſtrophe it was that the ghoſt ſtory was appended. Mademoiſelle Stéphanie de A—— was in Hungary when ſhe heard of the death of her *fiancé*, and for two years after, on her return to ——, ſhe wore

deep widow's weeds, and hence her *ſobriquet* of
" *la veuve.*"

One Chriſtmas Eve that I was to paſs at the
De A——'s I found Mélanie, the eldeſt of the
two ſiſters, alone, arranging the Chriſtmas tree.
As ſoon as the ſervant who had been helping her
to decorate it had aſked her when he ſhould
light up the little tapers about it, and had with-
drawn, after extolling her taſte, ſhe and I went
into the other drawing-room or reception-room,
and as we had it all to ourſelves we were no
ſooner ſeated in our reſpective *bergères* at each
ſide of the bright crackling pine fire, than I was
determined to lead up to the matter that was
preoccupying me; and after having broached the
ſubject of apparitions in general, and individual
viſitations in particular, I aſked her point-blank
if ſhe believed in ſuch things?

" *Comment! ſi j'y crois? Eh! mon Dieu! nous
en ſavons bien aſſez!*" was her reply, with a mo-
mentary ſhudder.

I then ventured ſo far as to ſay, that the *on dit*
at —— was, that her ſiſter had once ſeen a viſion
of ſome ſort.

She ſhook her head two or three times, ſlowly
but affirmatively. At length ſhe ſaid, after a ſhort
pauſe—

" *Ecoutez!* I believe Stéphanie likes you well
enough to tell you the hiſtory herſelf, and to-night,

when everyone is gone, I will try and get her to do so, and also to *show* you the proof of what she asserts. *Mais chut! la voici!*"

And as she spoke *la veuve* entered, and as soon after, the guests began to arrive, of course the conversation became general. But I resolved within myself that I wouldn't "go home till morning," if it were necessary, in order to hear the ghost story; in which expectation, I confess, the evening appeared unusually long, notwithstanding that I had the good fortune to win an *étui*, with a gold thimble, scissors, and needles, —most useful things in themselves, but to *me* rather in the category of what the sailors call "a watch-pocket for a cow." However, no matter how agreeable or how stupid a party may be, the time at length arrives when the comers must go. And go they did—all but myself. I was the last. I made a feint to follow the others, but Mélanie, proposing that "we three" should have a *bonne causerie* and some spiced wine, I, with a faint show of resistance, yielded to her *douce violence*.

" *Allons*," said she, " *racontez-nous, une de vos bonnes histoires.*"

I obeyed with the most amiable alacrity, and soon had both the sisters in fits of laughter. Mélanie then gave us an *impayable* anecdote of Madame de Staël-Holstein, which, though it did very well *en petit comité,* as *she* managed to tell it, would not exactly do for print, for we are *very* proper in *print*—we English, (would to goodness we were equally so in practice!).   At length it became the turn of Stéphanie to cater for our amusement. She began by excusing herself, saying she was so stupid that she really knew nothing worth our listening to.

"*Oh, que si!*" protested Mélanie; and rising and whispering something in her sister's ear, she added aloud, "*Oui, de grâce, ma bonne Stéphanie, je t'en prie!*"

And I adding my entreaties to hers, we at length prevailed upon her to narrate the following most extraordinary circumstance:

"I must tell you that about sixteen years ago, I was engaged to be married to M. Vanderveldt de Witt, of Amsterdam. Everything was arranged for the wedding to take place in a month, not in Holland but in Hungary, at the *château* of my friend, the Comtesse de G——, whom you have met here, and with whom I was then staying on a visit. It was late in October. I had on the morning of the 23rd received an *écrin* of very beautiful pearls and sapphires from my *fiancé,* and very kind letters from his mother and his sister Madame G—— de Z——. We were all in high spirits, and at supper (for in Hungary and Germany in those days people supped) the

Comte de G—— drank to the health of the future bride and bridegroom. A withered old diplomate, Baron von S——, alone refuſed to drink the toaſt, ſaying it was unlucky, and quoting the proverb, 'Many a ſlip 'tween the cup and the lip.'   As you may ſuppoſe, I thought this both unkind and ill-bred, and left the table in tears. Madame de G—— followed me up to my room, abuſing Baron von S——, who ſhe ſaid had always been an old *brouillon*, even in diplomacy, which only required head and no heart, and aſked me how I could be ſo ſilly as to let the croaking of ſuch a notorious old raven diſtreſs me, when I had had ſuch cheering and delightful letters that very morning, and would in one little month be able triumphantly to refute the Baron's beariſh growls?   I replied, 'Ah! what may not happen in or long before the expiration of a month, and I be none the wiſer?'[1]

" ' *Bah! eſt elle donc bête, cette petite fiancée?* ' was her only anſwer, and ſhe rang for Theckla, my *femme de chambre*, and tapping me on the cheek wiſhed me good night.   Now I muſt tell you that my bedroom was large and gloomy, an old wainſcoted room, with the bed in an alcove,

---

[1] There were neither railways nor electric telegraphs on any part of the Continent at that time, ſo that the tranſit of letters and all other news was ſlow, but by no means ſure.

as the beds in thofe old Hungarian *châteaux*
generally are; a good fire blazed on the hearth,
but not a fingle thing in the fhape of water, hot
or cold, in the room; for at the *inner* fide of the
alcove (in which the bed fitted as *clofely* as a
bracelet in a cafe) was a door opening into the
dreffing-room, where there was another fire, with
a kettle of hot water, and all the hip-baths,
bafins, cans of cold water, and other wafhing-
things; fo that had I wanted a glafs of water, or
firop, or *tifanne*, or anything, in the night, I muft
either have got out of bed and gone into the
dreffing-room for it, which was eafy, the door
opening from the wall, infide the bed, or have
rung for it; as, to fave my life, I could not at
either fide of the bed have had a table or chair,
however fmall, placed fo as to have had a cup or
glafs ftanding upon it.   You will fee as I go on,
that it was neceffary fully to explain this to you.
There was alfo of courfe *another* door into the
dreffing-room at the end of the room, *outfide* the
foot of the bed.   After I had wafhed and faid
my prayers, Theckla ftayed as ufual to put out
the candles, both in the bedroom and dreffing-
room, and then left me.   Tired out with the
excitement of the day, as well pleafurable as
painful, I fell afleep, and may have flept for
about an hour and a half, when I awoke with a
loud fcream, having dreamt that I faw Carle de

Witt fall into some deep black-looking water, that I had caught hold of him to try and save him, but his coat had given way, and he fell in with a terrific splash! and that was it, that woke me; but imagine my horror when, as if to prove it was a reality and no dream, I felt all the front of my nightgown, from the ankles to the shoulders, wringing wet and deadly cold! I rang the bell at the head of the bed violently, for I was so paralyzed between grief and fear that I could not get out of bed. Theckla appeared, as soon as she could get down out of her own room, with a shawl hastily thrown over her shoulders and her stockingless feet thrust into her slippers.

"'*Mon Dieu! est-ce que mademoiselle est malade?*' said she, hurrying to the bedside with the light.

"'For heaven's sake, Theckla, look here! What *can* this be?' said I, putting my hand upon her shoulder and getting out of bed; when both she and I, to our terror and astonishment, beheld my night things, not only splashed with a black muddy water from the ankles to the shoulders, but *dripping wet.*

"'*Seigneur Dieu!*' she exclaimed, 'what has happened to you?"

"I first told her to bring me another nightgown, and on *no* account to have the one I took off washed, but to let it dry, and put it carefully by.

I then told her my dream. She was so aghast that she made no attempt at refuting it, but kept on wringing her hands and turning up her eyes. I could not return to bed again, neither could I stand. I made Theckla bring pen, ink, and paper; I asked her to look at my watch and tell me exactly what o'clock it was; and allowing for the ten minutes that had elapsed from the time I had rang my bell to the time it had taken her to reach my room, and also allowing for the five additional minutes it had taken me to tell her my dream, I told her to write down in clear, large, legible letters (for my own hand trembled so much that I could not,) what I should dictate to her, and then to pin the statement to the nightgown and put them both carefully away. She accordingly wrote as follows, accompanying herself the while with innumerable "*Eh mon pères!*" and "*Est-il possibles!*"

"'On the night of the 23rd of October, 18—, Stéphanie de A— being at the *château* of the Comte de G— in Hungary, near ——, dreamt, at a quarter to twelve at night, that she saw M. Carle Vanderveldt de Witt's foot slip, and that he fell into some deep, black-looking water, nd athat she in vain tried to save him, when she awoke with the fright, and, wonderful to relate, found the front of her nightgown wringing wet, and splashed in a spiral and perpendicular direction, exactly as would have been the case had she been standing in it on the bank of a river and a heavy substance had fallen suddenly into the water.

"' Witnessed by me, THECKLA MORGANSTEIN,
at the Château de G——,
in Hungary, this night of the
23rd of October, 18—,
at half-past 12 at night.'

" I could not, as I have before said," continued Stéphanie, " return to bed the whole of that night, and the next morning I was in a brain fever; but as soon as letters could arrive from Holland, there came one to Madame de G—— from Marie de Witt (Madame G—— de Z——), to beg of her to break the fatal tidings to me. This letter bore the date of the 24th of October, and stated that on the previous day her brother Carle, had dined with her, and stayed late, talking over his future prospects and approaching marriage. As the night was very foggy, she wanted him to return home in her carriage, but he said he preferred walking. Passing one of the canals, the fog became so dense he could not see his hand before him, and stopping, it is supposed, to count the chimes of the Stadt House clock, then striking a quarter past twelve (at which hour his own watch was found to have stopped), on resuming his courſe, as is ſuppoſed by the man at the bridge, who heard the heavy ſplaſh, his foot ſlipped and he fell into the canal. Lanterns and flambeaux were immediately brought, but it was half-an-hour before the body could be found, and then it was quite dead.

" Seeing is believing," added Stéphanie, her voice almoſt inarticulate with emotion, as ſhe roſe, and taking a ſmall trefoil key out of her pocket, opened a drawer of an old carved oak *bahut*, or cabinet, and produced the nightgown, with the paper Theckla had written ſtill pinned to it. The dark ſplaſhes of foul, muddy water, exactly as ſhe had deſcribed, broad and heavy at the ſkirt from the hem, and tapering and ſprinkling in miry drops as the ſplaſh deſcended, was, without exception (under the circumſtances), the moſt extraordinary thing I ever ſaw in my life. After we had all three gazed on it for full five minutes in profound ſilence, ſhe took it, replaced it in the cabinet, put the key again in her pocket, and walked, without uttering a word, like a perſon in her ſleep, out of the room.

" *Pauvre Stéphanie !*" murmured her ſiſter.

" *Pauvre femme !*" ſighed I, as I preſſed Mélanie's hand, and quitted the houſe without any other adieux, to ponder on this ſtrange, but ower true tale.

Before I narrate the other ghoſt ſtory, which

was really an *apparition*, though in broad day-light, I may as well cite a few of Mr. Moreton's theories reſpecting apparitions.   After largely quoting from what he is good enough to call " Mr. Milton's fine poem," he next proceeds to turn the greater part of the " Paradiſe Loſt" into ſomewhat ludicrous proſe, deſcriptive of the Devil's innumerable metamorphoſes to tempt Eve ; he then goes on through all his (Satan's) various apparitions, as well as the celeſtial ones, throughout the Bible.

His claſſification of ſpirits is threefold; namely, angelic, or good ; demoniacal, or evil ; and the ſouls of living or dead men, which are not neceſ-ſarily either evil or good, but from being *ſpirit* and not matter, have perfect volition, and under peculiar and exceptional circumſtances, and the will of a higher power, perfect ubiquity.   And as an argument that our ſpirits, or, as they are called in Scripture, our " angels," may appear to others, when our ſtill living bodies are far diſtant, he inſtances Matthew xviii. 10, Chriſt's ſaying of little children, " *in heaven their angels do always behold the face of My Father which is in heaven.*"   And again, Acts xii. 15, when Peter knocked at the door where the diſciples were gathered together, and they, believing him to be in chains and in the priſon, ſaid, " *It is his angel.*"

He then goes on to ſay, while theoriſing on the poſſible nature and attributes of ſpirits—

"Others run out to an imaginary ſcheme of guardian angels attending every man and woman while they are upon earth; a notion ſo uncertain, if granted, and that has ſo many difficulties, that it is much better to leave it where it is, and which I ſhall explain preſently a much eaſier way.

"Now I ſay this is not my preſent buſineſs, to reconcile theſe diſtant and claſhing opinions, at leaſt not in this work. I have ſtarted a queſtion; poſſibly my opinion is with the affirmative, at leaſt I think it poſſible, and that it is rational to believe it; perhaps I may name you as improbable a notion, and much more inconſiſtent with the Chriſtian religion, which yet Philoſophy bids us call rational, and directs us to believe.

"How are we put to it, to form inhabitants for the planetary worlds! Philoſophy ſays they are habitable bodies, ſolid, opaque, as the earth, and we will have them be inhabited alſo, whether it be with or without, for or againſt, our reaſon and underſtanding; 'tis no ſatisfaction to them, or will it ſtop their cavils to ſay 'tis not a fact, that they are *not* habitable; that both *Saturn* and *Jupiter* are uncomfortably dark, and inſufferably cold, and would congeal the very ſoul (if that were poſſible), and ſo are not habitable on that account. That *Mercury* and *Venus* are intolerably hot, that the very water would always boil, and the fire burn up the vitals, and that in ſhort no human creatures could exiſt in ſuch heat. But this is not ſatisfactory neither, but rather than not have all theſe opaque worlds inhabited, and even their *Satellites*, or moons, about them too, they will have God be obliged to create a ſpecies of bodies ſuited to their ſeveral climates.

" In *Saturn* they are to live without eyes, or be as it were illuminated from their own internal heat and light, ſo as that they can ſee ſuccinctly from their own beams.[1]

" In *Jupiter* there muſt be another kind, who can live in twilight, and by the reflection of their own moons, and ſubſiſt in a continued froſt.[2]

" In *Mercury* the ſpecies muſt be all ſalamanders, and live in the continued fire of the ſun's rays, more intenſe than what would be ſufficient to burn all our houſes, and melt our iron, lead, and copper in the very mines. So that the inhabitants muſt be of a kind better able to bear

---

[1] Even in our little homœopathic globule of a planet, the earth, many perſons do this, and many more would be far better off if they would do the ſame. Only, unfortunately, thoſe who are illuminated from within, with us—can't.

[2] Theſe *we* have alſo in perfection.

fire than thoſe metals, and would ſtill live, though they were continually calcining or vitrifying.

"In *Venus* the heat would boil the water, and conſequently the blood in the body,[1] and a ſet of human bodies muſt be formed who could live always in a hot bath,[2] and neither fuſe out their ſouls nor melt their bodies.

"In *Mars*, ſo very dry in its nature, no vegetables or ſenſitives could ſubſiſt that we have any notion of, for want of moiſture; and the men that lived there muſt be dried up ſufficiently for pulverization on any ſuitable occaſion,—I mean human beings of our ſpecies.

"Now if God muſt not be ſuppoſed to have created ſo many habitable worlds without peopling them, and if it would reflect on his wiſdom to lay ſo much of His creation waſte that all the planets ſhould ſeem to be made for nothing but to range about the waſte, as a kind of dark inhabitants, of no uſe but to ſhine a little, and that with but borrowed luſtre[3] too,

---

[1] In our little planet, the earth, it is juſt the reverſe, for it is *ugly* things, more eſpecially what is emphatically called "*an ugly buſineſs*," that makes *our* blood boil.

[2] Here we Earthmen ſhow our ſuperiority again; for how many amongſt us there are who *do* live continually in hot water, and by the *laws* of our planet, are never out of it!

[3] Here again we Earthites beat them hollow; as we can, by innumerable modern inſtances, prove that ſuch a ſtate of

upon this little point called earth, where only a ſet of rationals[1] can exiſt,—I ſay, if this muſt not be ſuppoſed; but on the contrary, that there are certainly people of one kind or another in all theſe worlds, let the trouble of making them be what it will; if this be the caſe, and if this muſt be believed in ſpite of many difficulties and inconſiſtencies, then allow me to argue a little upon the following inquiry:

"Why may I not as well ſuggeſt, and that with every jot as much probability, that there are, or at leaſt may be, a certain number of appointed inhabitants in the vaſtly extended abyſs of ſpace, a kind of ſpirits (other than the angels, good or bad, and alſo other than the unbodied or uncaſed ſouls of men,) who dwell in the inviſible world, and in the vaſt *nowhere* of unbounded ſpace, of which we can neither ſay what it is, what it contains, nor how determined? That great waſte, of the extent of which, it is hardly poſſible even the ſoul itſelf can conceive, and of which all the accounts we give and the gueſſes we make, are ſo remote, look ſo enthuſiaſtic, ſo improbable, and ſo like impoſſible, that inſtead of informing the ignorant part of the world by it, we only arm them with jeſt and ridicule, and

---

luminouſly uſeleſs exiſtence (or, at leaſt, of no uſe but to the owner), is quite poſſible.

[1] Query, irrationals?

refolve them in incurable unbelief, depending
that what it is not poffible to conceive of is
not poffible to be.

"Now is this immenfe fpace indeed a void?
is it all a wafte? is it utterly defolate? or is it
peopled by the Omnipotent Maker in a manner
fuited to His own glory, and with fuch inhabitants as are fpiritual, invifible, and therefore
perfectly proper to the place?

" I muft needs fay 'tis more rational to fuggeft
this to be, than to bring out a fpecies of human
bodies to live in the intenfe heat of *Mercury* or the acute cold of *Jupiter* or *Saturn*.
The latter is agreeable to the general under-
ftanding we all have of fpiritual[1] beings. We
are all well affured that there are fome always
there, and that they can very well fubfift there;
that the place is fuitable to them, and that there
are fpirits of fome kind or other, and why not
fuch as we fuggeft?

" It remains then only to examine what com-
munication thefe fpirits have with us; whether
they are or are not able to hold converfation
with us, and whether they do converfe familiarly
with us, yea or no?"

---

[1] Or as Mr. Moreton calls them, "*fpirituous*" beings;
So that one would really fuppofe that he was writing of the
denizens of our own little planet before the advent of
Father Mathew.

" If it should be granted that there are such
spirits in existence, and that they pass and repass,
live, and have egress and regress there : that they
inhabit, as a certain bombastic author has it,

' Thro' all the liquid mazes of the sky,'

I say, if this should be granted, then it remains
that there is a fourth species that may assume
shapes ; for spirits can do that, and may appear
among us, may converse with our embodied
spirits, whether by dream, vision, or apparition,
or any superior way, such as to them, in their
great knowledge of things, may seem meet. To
speak as distinctly of this nice point as I can,
permit me to explain myself a little.

" If we grant that the spirit, though invisible
in itself, may assume shape, may vest itself so
with seeming flesh and blood as to form an
appearance, then all spirit may do it, since we
have no rule given us by which we may distinguish spirits one from the other ; I mean, as to
their actings in the capacity of spirits. We may
indeed, as I have said already, distinguish them
by the effect, that is to say, by the errand they
come on, and by the manner of their operations ;
as whether they are good or evil spirits ; but not
by their nature *as* spirit.

" The devil is as really a spirit, though a
degenerated, fallen, and evil spirit, I say he is as

much a ſpirit, to all the intents and purpoſes of a ſpirit that we are capable of judging of, as an angel. And he is called the Evil Spirit. He has inviſibility and multipreſence, as a ſpirit has; he can appear, though the doors be ſhut, and go out through them, though bolted and barred. No priſon can hold him, but his laſt eternal dungeon. No chain can bind him, but the chains faſtened on him by heaven, and the angel of the bottomleſs pit. No engine or human art can wound him. In ſhort, he is neither to be ſeen, felt, heard, or underſtood, unleſs he pleaſes; and he can make himſelf be both ſeen and heard too if he pleaſes; for he can aſſume the ſhape of man or beaſt, and in theſe ſhapes or appearances can make himſelf viſible to us, terrify and affright us, converſe in a friendly or a frightful manner with us, as he thinks fit. He can be a companion or a fellow-traveller in the day, an apparition or a horrible monſter in the night. In a word, he can be among us, and act upon and with us, viſibly or inviſibly, as he pleaſes, and as he finds to his purpoſe."

* * * * *

After reiterating this argument much in the ſame ſtrain, the author again cites the apparitions in ſacred hiſtory, pointing out and expatiating upon the grandeur or neceſſity of theſe angelic manifeſtations, and then adds, with much truth and ſome humour, with reſpect to the general run of vulgar ſuperſtitions and popular errors and fallacies—'But here you have an old woman dead, one it may be that has hid a little money in the orchard or garden, and an apparition is ſuppoſed to come and diſcover it, by leading the perſon it appears to to the place, and makes a ſignal that he ſhould dig there. Or a man is dead, and having left a legacy to ſo-and-ſo, the executor does not pay it, and then an apparition comes, and haunts this fraudulent executor till he does juſtice and pays it. Is it likely an angel ſhould be ſent from heaven to find out the old woman's earthen diſh, with thirty or forty ſhillings in it? Or that an angel ſhould be ſent to haraſs this man for a legacy of perhaps five or ten pounds? And as to the *Devil*, will any one charge *him* with being ſolicitous to have juſtice done? Thoſe who know him at all muſt know him better than to think ſo erroneouſly of him."

Another of his theories about the inviſible world is, that ſpirits are perhaps allowed to forewarn us of both coming good or evil and hence what we call "preſentiments;" but that they are not allowed to do more, that is, that they have no power to lead us actually out of evil or into good. At this rate, what would be the uſe of their myſtical tale-bearing?   And then again, what "mocking devils" ſome of theſe ſpirits muſt be,

> "Who never warn us till the deed is done!"

Mr. Moreton then waxes warm, grows ſatirical, touching the fops of his own times, and grows perfectly ſavage reſpecting the ancient and honourable order of "free and accepted Maſons." As I never belonged to the former, the ſtill more ancient, though leſs worſhipful order of Fops, I ſhall certainly not tarry to break lances for them; and as for the Freemaſons, their order has ſurvived all the quoits hurled at it by the malignant Moreton, and their good deeds and Chriſtian philanthropy as men are the beſt and moſt triumphant refutation of all calumnies againſt them, paſt, preſent, or future.   However,

> "Odioſa eſt oratio, cum rem agas longinquum loqui;"

So without any further beating about the buſh or digreſſion, I will juſt give one more extract from Andrew Moreton, as a curioſity of literature, and then proceed to "put in an appearance," *alias*, narrate my ſecond ghoſt ſtory.

"This hypotheſis of a ſuppoſed new claſs of ſpirits," ſays Moreton, "would lead me into a great many uſeful ſpeculations; and I might remark, with great advantages from it, upon the general indolence which it is evident has ſo fatally poſſeſſed our men of wit in this age. To ſee a fool, a fop, believe himſelf inspired! A fellow that waſhes his hands fifty times a day; but if he would be truly cleanly ſhould have his brains taken out and waſhed, his ſkull trepanned, and placed with the hind ſide before, that his under-ſtanding, which Nature placed by miſtake with the bottom upwards, may be ſet right, and his memory placed in a right poſition. To *this* un-ſcrewed engine talk of ſpirits and of the inviſible world, and of *his* converſing with unembodied foul, when he has hardly brains to converſe with anything but a barber or a powder puff, and owes it only to his being a fool that he does *not* converſe with the *Devil*, who, *if* he has any ſpirit about him, it muſt be one of thoſe indolent angels I ſpeak of; and if he has not been liſted among the infernals it has not been for want of wickedneſs, but only for want of wit.

" I DON'T wonder ſuch as thoſe go a mobbing among thoſe meaneſt of mad things called *Free-Maſons*; rough cheats and confeſſed deluſions are the fitteſt things to amuſe them. They are like thoſe fooliſh fiſh that are caught in large nets, that *might* get out at every ſquare meſh, but hang by the gills upon a mere thread, and chooſe to hamper and tangle themſelves when there is no occaſion for it, ſo that they are taken even in thoſe ſnares that are not laid for them.

"I now come to the main and moſt diſputed point of ſhadowy appearance, viz., the apparition of unembodied ſoul.

"It is a material difficulty here, and ought to be conſidered with the utmoſt plainneſs, viz., what we mean by *unbodied ſouls;* whether we underſtand by it ſouls which *have* been incaſed in fleſh, but being unhouſed are now moving about—in what ſtate we know not—and are to be ſpoken of in their ſeparate capacity; or whether there is any ſuch thing as A MASS OF SOUL, as a learned but inconſiſtent writer calls it, which is waiting to be embodied, as the ſuperior diſpoſer of that affair (be that who or what he pleaſes) may direct.

"This, I confeſs, is to me ſomething unintelligible, looks a little *Platonic,* and as if it were akin to the tranſmigration whimſey of the antients; but if they would found it upon anything rational, it muſt be on the ſuggeſtion mentioned above, viz. of a middle claſs of ſpirits, neither angelic-heavenly nor angelic-infernal, but ſpirits inhabiting the inviſible ſpaces, and allowed to act and appear here under expreſs and greatly ſtrained limitations, ſuch as are already deſcribed, and of which much more may ſtill be ſaid.

"But that I may clear up your doubt as to the point I am upon, I have added at the head of this ſection the word '*Departed,*' to intimate to you that I am orthodox in my notion, and that I am none of the sect of soul-sleepers, or for imprisoning souls in the *Limbus* of the antients; but that in a few words, by the appearance of souls unembodied, I mean such as, having been embodied or imprisoned in flesh, are discharged from that confinement, or, as I call it, unhoused, and turned out of possession; for I cannot agree that the soul is in the body as in a prison, but rather that, like a rich nobleman,[1] he [I thought the soul was feminine?] is pleased to inhabit a palace of his own building [!] where he resolves to live and enjoy himself, and does so, till by the fate of things, his fine palace being overturned, whether by earthquake or otherwise, is buried in its own ruins, and its noble owner turned out of possession without a house.

" This soul, we are told (and I concur in the opinion), has sometimes made a tour back into this world, whether earth, or the atmosphere of the earth—call it what you will, and express it how you will, it matters not much. Whence it comes, how far the journey, how and why it came hither, and above all, how it goes back again, and what those various apparitions are which

---

[1] Then how about those souls incarcerated in the suffering, struggling, starving bodies of poor beggars, and in those of (the worst sort of paupers) poor gentlemen and gentlewomen?

counterfeit theſe ſpirits,—enquire within, and you ſhall know farther.

" That the unembodied ſouls of dead men, or as we ſay, departed, *have* appeared, we have affirmed from the authority of Scripture, which I muſt allow to be an authentic document, whatever the reader may pleaſe to do, till a hiſtory more authentic and of better authority may be produced in the room of it."

In ſhort, Mr. Moreton goes on to prove, by many marvellous, well-authenticated hiſtories, that as we ſhould put on our cloaks or great coats for an airing, ſo diſembodied ſpirits ſometimes put on their bodies, or body coats, for a ſtroll back into this world, which, if they were wiſe ſouls, they would be only too glad to get out of, and be well rid of that cumbrous natural crinoline, the body. Though truly, the following hiſtory goes far to confirm Mr. Moreton's theory.

As I before premiſed, the chief actor in this moſt extraordinary apparition ſtory was by no means an imaginative, or even an impreſſionable perſon, nor yet a *raconteur;* he was ſimply a highly reſpectable paterfamilias, of ſtrict probity and ſcrupulous veracity, of middle age, and rather taciturn, when I knew him, or, it might be, ſobered by that moral ſoda-water, the cares of a large family, and that moſt ſedative of all fever draughts, high birth and low means. He had formerly been in a crack cavalry regiment, and winced, *tant ſoit peu,* as Mr. Moreton's "*great noblemen ſouls*" are apt to do when thruſt into a hovel inſtead of a palace of fleſh ; in fact, he did not like—who does ?—the change from the brocade to the huckaback of life; but he ſo far bowed to the rod as to take to it, and was ſo inveterate an angler and ſo keen a ſportſman that there was no diſtance too great for him to go, nor no trouble too much for him to take, for the chance of a bite ; he haunted every ſtream, and therefore knew the favourite haunts of every trout and grayling for miles round. I can well underſtand how either the meditative or the miſerable, are ſo fond of angling, were it only for the bleſſed practical wiſdom of the angler's motto—" I watch and I hope." But what I *don't* underſtand is, how, from being planted ſo long in the damp graſs, with a watery grave before them, and little fiſhes eternally popping up their heads open-mouthed againſt them, like thoſe in the enchanted frying-pan of the Arabian Nights—what I cannot underſtand, I ſay, is, that they don't get a chronic purſed-up mouth *en cœur,* like that of their patron ſaint, dear old Izaac Walton himſelf, as he has come *flâneur*-ing down to poſterity in that prim perch of a looking portrait that hangs out like a ſign at the frontiſpiece of his lives of Donne, Hooker, Sir Henry Wotton, George Herbert, &c., and where it is as palpable and patent, as if his wife had juſt whiſpered the fact to one, and that one *ſmelt* the lavender out of the drawer from which they had been taken—that that rigidly new doeſkin glove and thoſe two broad, maſſive, fine gold rings were not put on *every* day!—and a good thing too, for as Mr. Fact uſed to obſerve in Charles Matthews ſenior's inimitable *répertoire*, they'd "*frighten the fiſh!*" No, I'm not ſurpriſed at men whom that jade, Fortune, has jilted becoming anglers, for if they can but keep their fancies from vagabondiſing after "Shelſey cockles," "Chicheſter lobſters," "Arundel mullet," and "Amerly trout," what a dual leſſon of patience under diſappointment, and habits of ſtrict temperance may the Fordidge trout teach them! which ſaith Walton—"never afford an angler any ſport, but either live their time of being in the freſh water by their meat formerly gotten in the ſea, (not unlike the ſwallow or frog), or by the virtue of the freſh water only, or as the birds of paradiſe and the chameleons are ſaid to live, by the ſun and the air;"—which, as any pariſh beadle or overſeer, or even ariſtocratic philanthropiſt, can tell you, is preciſely the proper diet and allowance for poor, and more eſpecially for deſtitute, bipeds.   Then, none but thoſe who have tried it, know the ſoothing myſteries of ivy-juice; which, while it bewitches the fiſh, " cheers and *not* inebriates " the gentleman by whom, poor ſilly thing, ſhe is ſo taken.   But even the oldeſt angler in the world, HOPE! not only ceaſes to angle, but ceaſes to exiſt, when ſhe is quite ſure that the waters are ſo troubled that ſhe can catch nothing, various as her baits are: for ambition, power; for avarice, wealth; for love, phantom hearts, that in his own ſun-light *look* like golden ones, wreathed with chains of everlaſting flowers, which do admirably to ſtrew upon his own early grave; for poverty, guineas; and for indefatigable anglers, guiniads. Ah! whether we look down into the ſtream, which, like our life, is ever flowing from us, or up, into the heavens, which are eternally awaiting us—

> Hopes, what are ye? April ſhowers,
> A rainbow, for life's waiting hours;
> Bright tints that ſpan far diſtant ſpheres,
> All fading as that future nears!

Yet, ſweeteſt and gentleſt of all ſpirits, viſible or inviſible, ſiſter of charity of the heart, ministering angel of the mind—who ever dwelleſt with the poor and lowly, and bindeſt up the gaping wounds made by cruelty and injuſtice; who when we faint and writhe on earth whiſpereſt of Heaven;

who, when caſt away and tempeſt-toſt, faveſt us with thine anchor—think not that for worlds of realized happineſs I would be ſo impious as to breathe one diſparaging word of thee! For when at laſt thou leaveſt us, it is but in the ſpirit of truth, becauſe thou knoweſt that when Fate has left nothing to thee, there is no longer anything for us, and thou muſt of neceſſity give up thy garriſon; for when a life has been poiſoned, not only at every ſource, but through every channel, thou, with all thy bleſſed healing art, canſt only for a time mitigate ſuffering; thou canſt not give an effectual antidote; Death alone can do that. But ſo good, ſo kind, art thou, that the poor four-footed creatures thou leadeſt with a ſurer inſtinct than ourſelves, or elſe never would the poor Vicar have exclaimed, in (the moſt touching of all the records of one of God's ready-made angels) his journal :[1]

"Truly, there muſt be ſomething which attracts the unfortunate towards me; if anyone is in want he comes firſt to me—me! who have ſo little to give. I have remarked alſo, that when I am dining anywhere from home, and there is a dog in the houſe, it is on my knee that he always lays his cold noſe firſt in ſearch of a morſel."

---

[1] One of the moſt, not to ſay the moſt, charming ſtories ever written, "Journal of a Poor Vicar," by Henry Zſchokke.

But I ſee Colonel H. has got his baſket and all his fiſhing-tackle ready, and as to his varieties of bait, I rejoice that I am neither angler nor natu-raliſt enough to deſcribe them ; no doubt *he* had read every line of Ulyſſes Aldrovandus " De Piſcibus;" I have not, and I'll venture to ſay *you* have not either, Reader, which will give us the leſs to carry, ſo let us ſet out. There is no uſe in telling the world at large (which, I dareſay, has other fiſh to fry,) how in the brawling, bubbling, bounding Dee, Colonel H. broke one rod with a crafty old barbel. For, as Walton affirmeth, " the barbel affords the angler choice ſport, being a luſty and a cunning fiſh ; ſo luſty and cunning as to endanger the breaking of the angler's line by running his head forcibly towards any covert or hole in the bank, and then ſtriking at the line, to break it off with his tail ; as is obſerved by Plutarch in his ' De Induſtriâ Animalium ;' and alſo ſo cunning as to nibble off your worm cloſe to the hook, and yet avoid letting the hook come into his own mouth."

Bullied by this diplomatic old barbel, deter-mined to walk much further on towards a moun-tain (for it was in North Wales), to a quieter part of the river, where he knew the trout moſt did congregate, at length he walked ſo far, that he quite loſt his way ; but having had excellent ſport during the day, he had not, till the ſun began to fink into its gorgeous bed of crimfon and gold, remarked how far he had ftrayed out of his ufual beat. He began to look about him in queft of a road one way or the other, but above him was nothing but mountains, behind him interminable thickets of underwood and ftunted oak, and before him the fhallow river, where no coricle could have fkimmed, on account of the giant ftones fcattered in all directions and rifing from the bed of the river, always fhallow at this juncture in fummer: fo fhallow, that anyone as nimble as Colonel H. was might with eafe have croffed it by jumping from ftone to ftone, without ever wetting his feet. It however never entered his head juft at that time to think of croffing it; he was ravenoufly hungry—completely *déforienté*, not to fay *défarçonné*—and not a human being of whom, or even a human habitation where, he could have afked his way; no, nor even an intelligent fheep-dog, that can do better than fpeak—for they always act, and that fenfibly and effectually. The landfcape was ftill flooded with the glorious light of the departing fun, but ftill, above his golden diadem was one of thofe draperies of purple-black clouds which in mountainous countries are the fure heralds of a coming and fudden ftorm.

" Well, this is pleafant!" faid Colonel H., looking about him in all directions for at leaft the twentieth time. "What on earth am I to do ? I ſee no road in any direction ; and to go back, dodging along the river as I came, at this hour and a ſtorm coming on, would be madneſs." And again he aſked himſelf out loud what he was to do, without obtaining any more ſatisfactory anſwer. Then adding in his own mind, "I wonder, if I croſſed over to the other ſide, whether I ſhould find any ſort of a road ?" In order to do ſo, he ſtooped down to pick up ſome of his fiſhing tackle, and arrange it more compactly and portably on the top of his baſket. As he looked up from completing his packing he ſaw, ſtanding oppoſite to him, on one of the large ſtones in the centre of the bed of the river, an exceedingly pretty little girl between five and ſix years old, with dark blue eyes, bright golden hair, that fell from under a large round ſtraw hat in a profuſion of ringlets on her ſhoulders. She had on a little dark blue or purple bodice, with a bright red petticoat, little white ſocks, with black ſhoes buttoned round the ankle, with a ſtrap from the heel, ſuch as young children wear. But as ſhe ſtood, the ſun forming a complete halo round her, ſhe looked far more like a little opera *coryphée* than a peaſant's child.

After having gazed at her for about a ſecond in ſurpriſe and admiration, Colonel H. called out—

"Ho! I ſay, my pretty little girl! can you tell me if there is any road or houſe near this? There muſt be ſome houſe, or elſe you would not be here."

No anſwer. The child moved on, *how*, he could not tell, as ſhe certainly neither jumped nor made any other movement; ſtill, ſhe had advanced three or four ſtones further on, but kept looking back at him, not with what is generally denominated a ſmile, but ſomething more; it appeared like an irradiation from within, lighting up her whole face, without however any muſcular movement of the mouth or any other feature.

"'Pon my word," ſaid he, "you are a pretty, fantaſtic little creature! not a common child, evidently. I wonder who you are, and how they came to let you out by yourſelf, to take ſuch a dangerous ramble!"

And then he repeated his former queſtion in a louder voice.

Still no anſwer, but the child kept looking wiſtfully back at him.

"Do you mean that I ſhould follow you?" he aſked. She ſlightly nodded her head.

"Well, by Jove, I *will!*" cried he, jumping at once from ſtone to ſtone into the centre of the river, and trying to balance himſelf like a man on a tight-rope without a balancing pole. But by the time he had reached the ſecond large ſtone, where the child had ſtood, ſhe was again ſeveral yards in advance of him.

"Come, tell me your name, there's a good little girl?"

But ſhe only accelerated her pace—*how*, he could not tell, as, watch as cloſely as he would, or, rather, as he could, in the attention he was obliged to beſtow on his own ſtepping, he could not diſcover; but upon looking ſuddenly up after one of his own tranſits, he perceived ſhe was then at a conſiderable diſtance from him.

"Heyday! my dear little Will-o'-the-wiſp! this will never do. I really cannot get over the ground, or rather, over the ſtones, as you do."

The child pauſed, and remained perfectly motionleſs for about five minutes, till he had come up with her, to within a few yards, when he ſtretched out his hand, reſolved to clutch her dreſs, that ſhe ſhould not again eſcape him; but he only clutched the air, and ſhe was once more ever ſo far before him. And then again ſhe ſtood quite ſtill, to give him time to reach her; but, as before, in vain he tried to touch her, for in an inſtant ſhe was yards further.

In ſhort, this ſort of phantom chaſe continued for more than an hour, and extended over full three miles, the clouds gradually growing darker and more portentous, till at length a loud clap of thunder, accompanied by a vivid flaſh of lightning and a few large heavy drops, announced that the gathering ſtorm had culminated. Colonel H. was beginning to experience a degree of myſtification that almoſt amounted to fear, as he recalled all the wild legends of the Hartz and the Lurlei, and did not half reliſh the idea of *his* being ſelected as Goblin Maſter of the Revels, to take the initiative in introducing them into England, or at leaſt Wales, which was much the ſame thing. So ſuddenly ſtopping, he called out at the top of his voice—

"I tell you what, my little ſprite—elf, fairy, or whatever you are! I'm not going to be led this wildgooſe chaſe by you all night; ſo if you won't tell me your name, or at leaſt where you are going and what you want, I'll turn back,—which I was a precious fool not to have done long ago."

The child again ſtood perfectly ſtill, and looked back at him. She did not beckon, neither did ſhe fold her hands and hold them up, as if praying; but deep as the twilight now was, he could ſee the expreſſion of her face as clearly as if it had been noon; her very ſoul ſeemed, as it were, to be kneeling in her eyes, and ſaid more imploringly than any words could have done—

"Do, *pray do*, come on!" And in ſpite of himſelf, and without any volition in the matter, on he went, for it might be about another mile;

it was now quite dark, the rain falling in torrents, but his myſterious little leader was occaſionally revealed to him by a vivid flaſh of lightning. He by this time felt that ſort of reckleſs reſolution which may be termed the courage of deſpair, and he would not have turned back if he could; and ſtrange to ſay, now that he had ceaſed to ſee where he was going, and therefore carefully to pick his ſteps, he ſeemed to bound on with a ſort of involuntary and preternatural elaſticity. At length there came one broad vivid flaſh, that ſteeped the whole landſcape in flame for about a ſecond, and revealed to him, on the right-hand ſide of the river, a thickly-wooded mountain ſide, with a ſteep narrow ſheepwalk winding up it. Thither the child now darted, as uſual, firſt looking back at Colonel H. to follow,—a mandate which he had no longer either the power or the inclination to reſiſt; and he even experienced a ſort of phyſical relief at finding himſelf once more on *terra firma.* The rain by this time was coming down in ſuch rivulets, that it made that hiſſing, ſeething ſort of noiſe, which reſembles the ſhooting of cart-loads of gravel; and after about half-an-hour's more walking, or rather being propelled by ſome unaccountable impetus, he ſuddenly ſtopped, breathleſs, panting, and drenched to the ſkin, when another flaſh of electric fluid, leſs vivid, but more blue and lurid than the one which had difclofed the ſheep-walk at the foot of the mountain, now ſhowed him a ſmall cottage like a ſhepherd's hut, againſt the door of which, the little figure leant, and with a ſmile that was perfectly ſeraphic, beckoned to him, pointed to the door, and as he ſtretched out his hand to graſp hers immediately diſappeared! For a few ſeconds Colonel **H.** remained breath-lefs and ſtupefied, not well knowing whether his imagination had become the ſport of ſome fan-taſtic dream, or whether he was really a waking ſane man; at all events, the exhauſtion, and the wet, with which his clothes were ſaturated, were but too real. After wringing ſome of the water from his coat, he put out his hand in the direc-tion that a minute or two before, he had ſeen by the lightning was the cottage door, though half dreading that it would only again meet with empty air; but to his inexpreſſible relief it met with the ſolid reſiſtance of an oaken door, upon which he loſt no time in knocking loudly with his knuckles. No anſwer; or if there was one, the fierce loud conteſt between the wind and rain prevented his hearing it. So he knocked again, louder than before, and called out, " Any one within ? For the love of heaven open the door!" and before he had well ceafed ſpeaking, a bolt was drawn, and the ſharp click of an iron latch announced the opening of the door, at which an old woman, with one of thoſe dazzlingly white, well-ſtarched linen mob-caps that the Welſh peaſant women wear, and a grey plaid ſhawl over that again, (as a protection againſt the ſtorm,) appeared on the threſhold, and ſaid in Welſh, and in the uſual national high, ſhrill, quick key, " Is that you, Amos Price? it 's time for you, leaving me all theſe hours with what can never be company to me again, poor dead lamb! poor dead lamb! We had no buſineſs to make a king's child of her, as we did, and ſo God has taken her, as we made an angel of her."

The concluſion of this ſpeech was ſobbed out rather than ſpoken, and Colonel H., not waiting for an invitation, walked in, ſlammed to the door, and ſaid to the old woman, in as much Welſh as he could muſter, that he was not Amos Price, but an Engliſh gentleman, who had loſt his way in the mountains, and that if ſhe would allow him to dry his clothes, paſs the night on the oak bench beſide her fire, and dreſs him ſome trout for his ſupper (of which he had brought plenty) he would pay her well for her trouble.

The latter ſentence is one that never fails to be heard by the deafeſt Welſh ears and to touch even the hardeſt Welſh heart. So the old woman dropped a low curtſey, with a—

" Yes, ſure, ſir!" adding, " Eh! but *hur's* juſt *arownded!*" in her beſt Engliſh, proceeding to disencumber her unexpected guest of his coat and fishing-rods; after which she knelt down before the wood embers burning on the hearth, and blowing them with her breath, lit a rush-light, and from it, to do all honour to her visitor, a small lamp in a tin sconce, that hung above one of the oak settles inside the ponderous chimney; while a wooden screen of nearly black oak, divided into square compartments, like a window frame, and polished by time, projected from the right-hand side of the fireplace, to keep off the draught from the door and the window, as is common in old Welsh farm-houses and cottages. Meanwhile, Colonel H. took off his hat and coat, and asked the old woman to hang the latter on the back of a chair to dry; while she, perceiving by the light that he really was a gentleman, redoubled in her alacrity and civility, and while, according to his directions, she was taking the fish out of the basket, said—

" I'm sure I beg *hur* pardon, but I thought te was my old man come back."

And here she put the corner of her apron to her eyes and sighed deeply.

Colonel H., pre-occupied with his strange adventure, flung himself into the oak settle inside the warm old chimney corner, and stretching his feet to the full length of it (first having taken off his boots and put them to dry against one of the iron dogs), while he gazed liſtleſſly at the fire for a few ſeconds, experienced that luxurious *dolce far niente* which a reclining poſition after extreme fatigue always ſuperinduces. Meanwhile, the old woman beſtirred herſelf, and laid a clean, coarſe, unbleached cloth on a little round table, with knife, fork, pepper, ſalt, and a brown loaf, and having put two plates againſt the other iron dog oppoſite the boots to get hot, reached down a fryingpan from among ſome bright tin ſaucepan covers, and a ſmall braſs peſtle and mortar that graced the mantlepiece. And it was not till Colonel H. heard the welcome ſounds of the trout being initiated into the habits of civilized life, that he was rouſed from his reverie, and half ſtarting up, ſaid—

"I'm ſure I'm very much obliged to you! I'm ſorry to give you ſo much trouble. Can I help you?"

"Ha, ha! *te* ain't no trouble; put hur ſorry hur ain't cot no pier, nor cider, nor nothing put water."

"Never mind," ſaid her gueſt, laughing, and rubbing his hands, as ſhe now transferred the trout to a hot diſh and placed it on the table; "Never mind, for my ſpeckled friends, here are all temperance people, and never touch anything elſe; but if you will be ſo good as to give me a glaſs of water, I'll drink your and their health, for I'm choking with thirſt."

After he had fulfilled his promife and pledged the old woman, **H.** bowed to the trout, and faid—

"Gentlemen, here's to you! I'm charmed to fee you, but as *l'éloge fe fait en mangeant*, I'll foon prove my fincerity," and cutting a thick piece off the brown loaf, he foon began to eat, as men do eat, who have walked and fafted nearer twelve hours than ten. As foon as his hunger was in fome degree appeafed, *viâ* a fecond *entrée* of the fame difh, he afked the name of his prefent whereabout. The old woman told him fome unpronounceable Welfh name, which got entangled in the burr in her throat and left him as wife as he was before. Fortunately, he was in the habit, on his fifhing expeditions, of fleeping at little village inns, fo that his family, knowing how far his favourite paftime led him, would not be alarmed at his abfence on the prefent occafion; ftill, being determined to return as early as poffible in the morning, he now afked his hoftefs how far they were from ——? She told him fifteen miles.

"Whew!" faid he, giving a long whiftle, deadly tired as he was that night, and having to pafs it without a bed, not much relifhing the idea of fo long a walk before breakfaft. "I wonder," faid he, "you are not afraid to live in fuch a lonely place."

"What would we have to be te feared of?

Poor people like us have no need to be te feared te thieves.”

“ Well, I don’t exactly mean thieves; but witches and ghoſts, and that ſort of thing.”

“ Eh ! te was only in old times there was ſuch things as them ; there ain’t none now.”

“ What? out of ſeaſon, eh ? like green peas at Chriſtmas.　So you have no faith in ſpirits ? ”

“ If my old man was te home he could get hur *ſperits* at the ‘ Queen’s Head,’ but we ha’nt none.”

Colonel H. ſmiled, and aſſured her he would not trouble her old man for any ſuch purpoſe.　He then ſaid, looking up at her bright array over the mantlepiece, “ You have a ſnug little nook of it here, and you keep it very nicely, which is the whole ſecret of making any place nice or the reverſe, be it a palace or a hovel.”

And then he caſt a look all round.　Oppoſite to him was what he ſuppoſed to be a bed in a receſs, by the blue and white checked curtains, with plaited valance at the top that was drawn before it.　When, as his eyes travelled round, and reſted on the wall oppoſite the large fireplace, upon which an additional faggot now made a cheerful blaze, his cheek blanched and he gave a ſudden ſtart ; for there he ſaw hanging up, *the* little red petticoat, blue bodice, and large round ſtraw hat, that the phantom child who had lured him to the cottage had worn! while, that no ſingle identification might be wanted, on a table underneath them, on the top of a large Bible, were placed the little black kid ſhoes and a pair of white ſocks.

"Good heavens!" ſaid he, addreſſing the old woman, as he felt the cold drops of terror ſtanding on his forehead, while he pointed to them, " To whom do thoſe little clothes belong ?"

The old woman ſank down into a low chair, and covering her face with her hands, and rocking herſelf backwards and forwards, ſobbed out—

" They did belong to our little Amy, but *ſhe'll* never put them on again; ſhe's with the angels now, and it's juſt to the Vicarage at —— that Amos Price is gone, to tell the daughter of the Vicarage [1] how it happened ; and as ſhe was ſo fond of the poor little ſoul, and taught her to read, and all her pretty ways—too pretty, it ſeems, for this world!—to ſee if ſhe could not get enough

---

[1] In North Wales the common people ſeldom give perſons their proper name, but generally call them by that of the name of the houſe, or even of the ſign of the public-houſe, where they live ; ſo that it is a common thing to hear a publican's ſon deſignated by the Oſſianic and grandiloquent title of " the Son of the Eagle," or his daughter, by the Oriental one of " the Daughter of the Moon ;" and it is always the ſon or daughter " of the vicarage," and never " of the vicar."

from the gentlefolks, that uſed to be good to her, to put up a ſtone to her; for I ſhould be ſorry for her little grave to be loſt in nettles and weeds— ſhe that was ſo fond of flowers, and brought home ſuch a frockful from the mountain the very day before. But I've put 'em all ready for her to take with her. My old man ſaid it was nonſenſe, for there were better flowers in Heaven; but hur loved thoſe while hur was here, and hur *ſhall* have them." And here the poor old creature went off into a violent paroxyſm of hyſterics.

Colonel H. roſe and brought her a glaſs of water, and ſaid to her ſoothingly,—for indeed the tears were in his eyes, as he thought, although thoſe who had loved poor little Amy would never ſee her in her bright little fantaſtic dreſs again, how recently and ſtrangely he had done ſo; though there it hung, at once myſtifying, baffling, and confounding his reaſon, on that white wall before him,—yea, almoſt tenderly, he ſaid to her, for he ſpake from his heart—

"Don't fret yourſelf about a tombſtone for your little Amy; I'll take care that ſhe has one as pretty as herſelf."

"Cot pleſs hur! I'm ſure, ſir, I thank hur kindly. Ah, ſhe *was* pretty! You would have ſaid ſo, ſir, but you never ſaw her."

He did not care to contradict her, and ſo merely ſaid—

" Poor little thing, ſhe was your child ?"

" Grandchild, ſir."

And again the old woman covered her face, and rocked herſelf to and fro.

" Ah, I ſuppoſe her parents are away ?" probed Colonel H., his curioſity excited to know how the very commonplace old peaſant woman before him could be really the grandmother of ſo beauti-ful and poetical looking a child.

" Parents, indeed !" muttered the old woman.

" What? ſhe hadn't any?   Both dead ?"

" Yes, yes ; ſhe had a mother, *my* child, worſe luck!   She was as pretty as Amy.   It's a great curſe, a great ſnare, ſir, is beauty !"

And here ſhe burſt into a freſh paroxyſm of tears.   Colonel H. perceived there was ſome painful hiatus in the child's parentage, and was at no loſs to fill it up.   So not additionally to diſtreſs the poor old woman by again alluding to this point, he merely ſaid—

" When did your poor little Amy die ? "

" Only yeſterday, ſir."

" Dear me, how ſad !   Was ſhe long ill ?"

" No, no !—*drownded, drownded !* "

And again ſhe rocked herſelf backwards and forwards, in uncontrollable grief.   At length ſhe ſaid, looking up at him—

" Do look at her, ſir ; it's not like death, it's juſt like a piĉter."

And taking the lamp from out of the chimney ſhe walked to the bed and drew aſide the curtain, when to Colonel H.'s ineffable ſurpriſe, and not without a cold ſhudder running through his very marrow, he beheld—as if in that calm and profound ſleep which only children know, and which, from its peaceful beauty, angels may well be ſuppoſed, not only to watch over, but to whiſper every dream that haunts it—yes, there he beheld the little figure that had ſo long flitted before him and lured him to the cottage! the rich maſſes of her ſilken hair ſhading her beautiful face, and falling like ſhowers of rippling gold againſt the marble of her cheeks and the ſnowy whiteneſs of her little night-dreſs, while the little hands were folded on her boſom ; and placed under them, and ſupported by her cheſt, ſince the muſcles that death had relaxed could no longer hold them, was a bunch of faded wild flowers, the very laſt, as the old woman informed him, that ſhe had gathered the morning of her death, a few hours before ſhe had fallen into the river.

Colonel H. felt a choking, ſuffocating ſenſation in his throat and a moiſture in his eyes that made him want to get into the air ; and yet, as he honeſtly confeſſed to me, he did not like venturing to leave the cottage alone.

"Poor little Amy !" ſaid he, "you were indeed

beautiful! but you are better off now, for you are where you will never be lefs fo."

He gently drew the curtain, turned away from the bed, put a fovereign into the woman's hand, and afked her where fhe intended to have the child buried, for, as he before told her, he would take care fhe fhould have a fuitable monument, for which the old woman was profufe in her bleffings and thanks. He then afked her if there was no village near, where he could procure any fort of conveyance to return by that night. She faid, " Yes, at Llantys" fomething, where the Vicarage was fituated, which was only two miles from thence; and that when Amos Price returned he fhould fhow him the way.

So, defpite his impatience to be gone, as the ftorm had now ceafed and the moon was fhining brilliantly, he was fain to wait patiently for another hour, till the old man came back.

This ftrange ftory I tell as it was told to me. In the ftrict veracity of the chief actor in it, who narrated it to me, I have implicit faith, knowing it to be unimpeachable. As to explaining fuch things, that is beyond mortal ken; and though *cui bono*-ing them may prove our ignorance, it cannot enlighten it. But of this I am convinced, that our intelligence, when even of the moft exalted nature of which humanity is capable, is, by an all-wife Omnipotence, advifedly made finite; for if " by fearching we *could* find out," or by fpeculating we *could* foar to, and penetrate the myfteries of the infinite, not *one* of us, from the monarch who beftows honours, to the mendicant who begs alms, would or could, for even a fingle hour, go his circumfcribed and monotonous rounds in *the* particular mill allotted to each of us, and which, however apparently and comparatively infignificant, is as *abfolutely* neceffary to the vaft machinery of God's concrete and complex creation as A WHOLE, and the progreffive working out of its ultimate defign, as are the broad bafis, or the all-important axis, of

" THE GREAT GLOBE ITSELF."

And now, Reader, once more farewell ! This is an archæological and curiofity-feeking age. In the hope of amufing you through an idle hour, I have placed before you a few quaint old things from the Regalia of Remphan, which are not to be found even in the right good collection of the South Kenfington Mufeum. If they are not fortunate enough to pleafe you, the fault is not wholly mine, becaufe the matter is not wholly mine ; I have only been a bad purveyor, of which there are but too many in this utilitarian age. I can, therefore, but confcientioufly affure you that

I have adulterated none of the articles, but have given them to you genuine as I imported them.

Fabian, Speed, Stow, Sir Matthew Hale, Camden, and Bishop Fleetwood (the latter in his "Chronicon Preciosum"), all tell us that up to the reign of John both the bold barons and the monks were allowed to coin their own money [1] —delightful privilege! which they so abused that at length it was rescinded [2] (an abuse which perhaps in the present day sometimes extends to authors in the habit of coining their own books). So that this right, at length became vested solely in the Crown, the consequence of which was, that each reign had a different coinage peculiar to itself. From the mancas of the Saxons, to the

---

[1] But even after they were deprived of this privilege the Crown occasionally, by various charters and grants, allowed several bishoprics and abbeys the right to erect a mint within their own jurisdiction, and there to coin their own money; such as the Abbot of St. Edmund's Bury, the Archbishop of York, and the Bishop of Durham. But they had not the domination of stamp or alloy. Camden mentions having seen some copper coinage of the time of Claudius Cæsar, struck in London, and bearing the inscription *Pecunia Londoni Signata*, and others when London was called Augusta, with that of *Præpositus Thesaurorum Augustantium*, namely, "The treasurer of the mint of Augusta," or London.

[2] It was Henry II., not John, that put a stop to this coining usurpation of the baronage. He coined new money, and ordained that none other but what issued from the royal mint should pass current throughout his kingdom.

mark of the Middle Ages, the groffus or groat,[1] the filver penny, (firft weighed againft wheat grains), the Efterlings, as they were called, the *oboli* (galley-pence—fo called from being imported from Genoa, with which we had once great trade), the crocards or cocodines and rofaries (all afterwards called in by Elizabeth), the falutes or angels (ftruck in France by Henry V., and made current in England), the pollards, ftepings, ftaldings, fufkins, blanks of Henry VII., the dandypratts and the doitkins (alfo ftruck by Henry V., and from this latter comes our to this day current expreffion of " not worth a doit"), the deep, rough, indented croffed coin of the Conqueror, made fo deep as to be eafily broken in halves or quarters for purpofes of traffic, before halfpence and farthings were invented ; the gold halfpennies and farthings (!) of Edward III.[2] and

---

[1] In 1378 a groat, or 4*d.*, was paid to the king for every man and woman ;—a very pretty little poll-tax, and hence, no doubt, the origin of the faying, " Not worth a groat," which, poor creatures, it may be fuppofed one-half of them were not, either in a moral or monetary point of view.

[2] According to Fabian, Edward III. it was, who firft caufed farthings and halfpennies to be coined *round*, and as a feparate coin, for till then the croffed coin of William the Conqueror, had been broken into halves and quadrantes, or farthings ; and Fabian gives the following piece of " poetry " as he calls it, made at the time to commemorate the *royal* invention :—

Richard II., the angels, rofe nobles, and fpur royals of Elizabeth and James I.'s times; the Commonwealth crowns, with their Pharifaical motto of "GOD WITH US;" yea verily! from the firft coin ftruck by Prince Cunobeline,[1] ruler of the Trinobantes, before which the ancient Britons, lacking fpecie of any kind, trafficked with rings of iron[2] and plates of brafs—*all* have had their day, down to the fovereign of our own times.

So have I given you, Reader, the coinage of many minds, and if the black mail or copper currency has not been *all* called in, I hope you will at leaft find amongft it, one or two gold farthings.

"EDWARD did fmite round penny, halfpenny, farthing,
The Croffe paffes the bond of all throughout the ring;
The king's fide was his head, and his name in written,
The Croffe fide what city it was in coyned and fmitten.
To poor man, ne to prieft, the penny frayeth nothing.
Men give God ay the leaft, they feaft him with a farthing.
A thoufand, two hundred, four fcore years and mo,
On this money, men wondered, when it firft began to goe."

[1] This Prince Cunobeline lived, according to Stow, at Camalodunum, now called Malden, in Effex, and flourifhed about the time of Julius Cæfar, in imitation of whom, he had his own image ftamped upon this coin,—the firft ever made in England, and ftruck at Malden.

[2] Speed fays that he himfelf had feen dug out of the earth, in little crufes or pitchers, thefe rings and brafs plates, the fubftitutes for coin of the ancient Britons.

For Her Own Good – A Series of Conduct Books

Cœlebs in Search of a Wife
Hannah More
With a new introduction by Mary Waldron
ISBN 1 85506 383 2 : 288pp : 1808–9 edition : £14.75

Female Replies to Swetnam the Woman-Hater
Various
With a new introduction by Charles Butler
ISBN 1 85506 379 4 : 336pp : 1615–20 edition : £15.75

A Complete Collection of Genteel and Ingenious Conversation
Jonathan Swift
With a new introduction by the Rt Hon. Michael Foot
ISBN 1 85506 380 8 : 224pp : 1755 edition : £13.75

Thoughts on the Education of Daughters
Mary Wollstonecraft
With a new introduction by Janet Todd
ISBN 1 85506 381 6 : 192pp : 1787 edition : £13.75

The Young Lady's Pocket Library, or Parental Monitor
Various
With a new introduction by Vivien Jones
ISBN 1 85506 382 4 : 352pp : 1790 edition : £15.75

Also available as a *5* volume set : ISBN 1 85506 378 6
Special Set Price: £65.00

Subversive Women

The Art of Ingeniously Tormenting
Jane Collier
With a new introduction by Judith Hawley
ISBN 1 8556 246 1 : 292pp : 1757 edition : £14.75

Appeal of One Half the Human Race, Women, Against the Pretensions of the Other Half, Men, to Retain them in Political, and thence in Civil and Domestic, Slavery
William Thompson and Anna Wheeler
With a new introduction by the Rt Hon. Michael Foot and Marie Mulvey Roberts
ISBN 1 85506 247 X : 256pp : 1825 edition : £14.75

A Blighted Life: A True Story
Rosina Bulwer Lytton
With a new introduction by Marie Mulvey Roberts
ISBN 1 85506 248 8 : 178pp : 1880 edition : £10.75

The Beth Book
Sarah Grand
With a new introduction by Sally Mitchell
ISBN 1 85506 249 6 : 560pp : 1897 edition : £18.75

The Journal of a Feminist
Elsie Clews Parsons
With a new introduction and notes by Margaret C. Jones
ISBN 1 85506 250 X : 142pp : New edition : £12.75

Also available as a 5 volume set : ISBN 1 85506 261 5
Special set price : £65.00